TODAY I F*****D UP

A hilarious collection of worst day disasters

Thomas Mitchell

SIMON & SCHUSTER

London · New York · Sydney · Toronto · New Delhi

Out of fairness to those f***-ups who requested it, some names and details have been changed in this book.

TODAY I F****ED UP: A HILARIOUS COLLECTION
OF WORST DAY DISASTERS
First published in Australia in 2021 by
Simon & Schuster (Australia) Pty Limited
Suite 19A, Level 1, Building C, 450 Miller Street, Cammeray, NSW 2062

10 9 8 7 6 5 4 3 2 1

Sydney New York London Toronto New Delhi
Visit our website at www.simonandschuster.com.au

© Thomas Mitchell 2021

All rights reserved. No part of this publication may be reproduced, stored in a retrieval system, or transmitted in any form or by any means, electronic, mechanical, photocopying, recording or otherwise, without prior permission of the publisher.

A catalogue record for this book is available from the National Library of Australia

ISBN: 9781760859039
Cover and internal design: Meng Koach
Cover image: Lawrence Furzey
Typeset by Midland Typesetters, Australia
Printed and bound in Australia by Griffin Press

MIX
Paper from responsible sources
FSC® C009448

The paper this book is printed on is certified against the Forest Stewardship Council® Standards. Griffin Press holds FSC® chain of custody certification SGS-COC-005088. FSC® promotes environmentally responsible, socially beneficial and economically viable management of the world's forests

To my wife, Kate, and her grandfather Ian – without either of you, this book would never exist.

Contents

Introduction: Damage, Joy	1
Where Does Grandad Keep His Guns?	9
THE FUCK-UP HALL OF FAME: Rotten Apple	25
We May Need to Amputate	28
THE FUCK-UP HALL OF FAME: The Unluckiest Man in the Luckiest Village	47
We Are Family	50
THE FUCK-UP HALL OF FAME: An Expensive Case of Elbow Painting	71
Lost My Mind (and Everything Else) in Madrid	74
THE FUCK-UP HALL OF FAME: Almost a Beatle	95
The Flight from Hell	98
THE FUCK-UP HALL OF FAME: To Pee or Not to Pee	121
You Can't Handle the Tooth	124
THE FUCK-UP HALL OF FAME: Loyal to a Fault	140
All I Want For Christmas Is a Do-Over	143
THE FUCK-UP HALL OF FAME: Hard Act to Follow	160
The Art of Disappointing Your Parents	163
THE FUCK-UP HALL OF FAME: Crash into (and All Over) Me	187
Do You See What I See?	191
THE FUCK-UP HALL OF FAME: Death by Delayed Bullet	215
Shit Happens	218
THE FUCK-UP HALL OF FAME: Emu Warfare	245
Acknowledgments	249
About the Author	250

Introduction

Damage, Joy

Growing up, there are few more volatile environments than the family road trip. No one wants to be there, no one is having fun and it never feels like a holiday. When I was young, my parents would try to jazz up the school break by stuffing my brother, sister and me into the Camry and driving us ten hours to somewhere that looked much like where we lived. Then for the next five, seven or ten days they would encourage us to do activities that usually involved being far away from them.

'Why don't you guys go exploring?' our mother would say, the boxed wine already sweating in the sun.

Now anyone with siblings will tell you that the relationship typically has two speeds: best friends or worst enemies.

But I had the unique problem that my brother and sister were twins, which made for a curious dynamic.

On some days I was an easy target. As the youngest you're born on the outer, and in any games we played to amuse ourselves I was inevitably cast in the least desirable role.

'Let's play piggy in the middle,' bossed my sister and, without being told, I would waddle to the middle, accepting my sad piggy fate. But on other days I became the swing vote as my brother and sister desperately vied to be top dog.

Each would approach me separately, seeking my backing and, because I was just happy to be included, whoever reached me first had my allegiance. We would then cruelly turn on the other person. Ha-ha! Feel the wrath of the piggy!

All this push-pull for power usually resulted in fighting, until my mother was forced to intervene. 'Do you think I want to referee your fights while I'm trying to enjoy my holiday?' she would ask, unwittingly making herself the common enemy.

I recall one particular trip where the bickering reached an all-time high. My father had decided to take us camping on the mid-north coast of New South Wales, which was a considerable dice roll because we were not campers. None of

INTRODUCTION

us really enjoy the great outdoors, so it was a tense week full of mosquito bites, wet socks and lost tent pegs. I was eight years old at the time and even then I remember thinking: 'We're *really* more of a resort family.'

By the time my parents were passive aggressively packing the car to leave, it was a proper pressure cooker. My brother and sister were no longer talking because of a disagreement on who was older. They had been born forty-five minutes apart, but no one could ever agree on who came out first. It remains a sore point to this day.

Meanwhile, my dad was dealing with the dual shame of being both in pain and embarrassed. During the camping trip, he'd been bitten by a spider, leaving a nasty welt on his leg. My father is many things, but a quiet sufferer is not one of them.

'Do you think it's infected?' he asked me, his eight-year-old son, shortly after it happened. I simply nodded.

Because of his infected bite, he struggled to pack the tent up – though I suspect he didn't know how to anyway – so a father from a nearby campsite offered to lend a hand. He was tall and strapping, the kind of man who could be bitten by many spiders and not think to mention it.

As NewDad expertly packed the tent away, OldDad moodily picked at his wound and shuffled off to the car. My mother found this whole episode amusing, and she used every opportunity to bring it up on the drive home.

This was, of course, a deliberate niggle designed to get a reaction. She hadn't escaped the dark cloud of this family getaway either and she too was fuming, mostly at my father for deciding camping was a good idea.

As we silently sped home, bad vibes were brewing in the car and even as kids, we knew it was safest not to break the quiet. Simon & Garfunkel bled out of the speakers while I shifted uncomfortably in the middle seat – another downside to being the youngest was a childhood of giving up the window.

About two hours into the journey, we hit a set of traffic lights, unusual for these quiet country roads. Minutes passed and nothing changed; the light remained red and so too did my father's face.

Laughing was definitely not allowed, but there was something comical about idling at a red on an empty road. As if the traffic gods had decided to test our patience.

While we played the waiting game, a white convertible with a retractable roof pulled up alongside us. I could feel my family's collective gaze drift towards the car, and I knew we were all thinking the same thing: *wow, a convertible.*

Despite being smack bang in the middle of the middle class, we were still impressed by any sniff of status. People who owned convertibles, along with people who had swimming pools, were the kind of people we aspired to be.

In response to the strange family staring at her, the woman behind the wheel pressed a button and the roof magically folded in on itself and disappeared. 'Woah,' I said, finally breaking the long silence – now she was just showing off.

She threw her head back and laughed, and while it didn't register at the time, she was probably laughing at us. We were the ogling battlers in the Camry, a sedan overloaded with tents and tension. She was living the high life in her flashy drop-top with the acrobatic roof and obnoxiously loud engine.

Unfortunately for her, it was this very engine that was to blame for what came next. She gave the motor an unnecessary rev, which was enough to spook a large pigeon from a nearby tree.

The bird took flight, cutting a path directly over her open car roof while being sure to drop an enormous turd from a great height. Had she not been laughing so heartily in our direction, her mouth would have been closed, but instead, it was wide open – a direct hit.

Our car exploded with the kind of laughter that is impossible to control, not that you'd want to. The more we looked at each other, the more we laughed, while our friend in the convertible gagged and spluttered.

Eventually, we heard the mechanical grunt of the roof closing, and that set us off once more. Quick, close the roof before he strikes again!

The light turned green, and my father hit the gas, leaving everything behind us. It no longer mattered which twin was older, or if I was piggy in the middle, or that my dad didn't know how to pack up a tent.

Our collective joy at witnessing this perfectly timed pigeon shit had wiped the slate clean.

I immediately understood the unique healing power that can be found in other people's misfortune.

Turns out there's a word for this feeling. Actually, there are a few words.

The ancient Greeks called it *epichairekakia*, while in French they refer to *joie maligne* or malignant joy. But perhaps the most famous of all is 'schadenfreude' – a compound of the German nouns *Schaden*, meaning 'damage' and *Freude*, meaning 'joy'. So satisfying is the sound of 'schadenfreude' we never bothered with an English translation, instead adopting the German as our own.

Schadenfreude, the act of deriving pleasure in another's pain and suffering, is not a new phenomenon. Stroll any gallery and you'll see artworks from every century depicting scenes of delight amid disaster.

Schadenfreude is everywhere. I spent half my childhood

INTRODUCTION

watching *America's Funniest Home Videos*, which is essentially schadenfreude on steroids. Endless clips of old people falling over and outrageous waterskiing accidents bundled together and broadcast for our entertainment.

It's no different these days, the internet only serving to increase our appetite for funny fuck-ups. Cat videos have been usurped by *catastrophe* videos, with Epic Fail compilations racking up millions of views on YouTube.

We are addicted to the downfall of our fellow humans, regardless of time, place or race.

And if there was ever a point in history that we all needed a little *joy* amongst the *damage*, it's now, in the age of divisive politics and global pandemics.

Which is why I decided to write this book of great stories about bad days. I convinced a bunch of people to share their most glorious fuck-ups of all time, and the result is a mixed bag of true tales that are both hilarious and horrifying.

In the following pages, I creatively retell their stories as a reminder that no matter how terrible things get, it could always be worse. Way worse. And of course, I include my own nightmarish bad day, because if I'm going to laugh at others, well, it's only fair that they laugh at me too.

Buckle up.

Where Does Grandad Keep His Guns?

Thomas's story

The minute we pulled into the long driveway that led to the house, I knew I was out of my depth. In the distance a ute kicked into gear and a big plume of dust filled the air as it sped towards us. Dust and dirt caked the car, getting into every crevice. I was already sneezing. Get me back to the city.

'Are you okay?' Kate asked in a way that meant she knew I wasn't okay, which made her even less okay.

'Yes,' I said, eyes watering. 'All good here.'

This was a trip two years in the making. On our first date, she told me her favourite place in the world was her grandparents' farm, a sprawling property called Balboora, an hour outside Dubbo, New South Wales. It was where she had spent every summer while growing up; all her important childhood memories had happened on the very land we were now driving across.

'That's where I learnt to ride a bike,' she said, pointing to a dirt trail on our left. 'And that's where I killed my first chicken.'

Kate had later asked me where my favourite place was and I'd lied and told her it was my father's village in Greece. I'd only visited the village once, as an eleven-year-old. My siblings and I spent most of the time complaining about the heat while a distant relative pointed out ruined buildings from his past. My actual favourite place was Death by Chocolate, a chocolate shop near my childhood home, where they gave out generously sized taste-testers and didn't mind if you took seconds.

Not only was the farm special to Kate, but her grandparents' tick of approval meant everything. Ian and Betty O'Connor were the gold standard of grandparents, the type to never let a birthday go by without sending a handwritten card and slipping a crisp fifty-dollar note inside.

Their regular phone calls were a highlight of Kate's week and she would take them in another room in order to safely adopt her country persona.

'G'day Grandad, how are ya?' she'd yell, dropping syllables all over the place. 'I'm missin' ya, I'll tell ya that much!'

The closer we got to the house, the more countrified Kate became, winding down her window to take it all in. 'The air smells different out here don't ya reckon?' she asked. I sniffed but couldn't tell the difference.

Much of the drive from the airport had been an intense study in what not to do once we arrived.

'Don't leave the fridge open, Grandad hates that and it will set him off. Don't leave the table before Grandad does, it's a respect thing. Don't shower indoors: that's for girls only; boys shower outside. And don't shower for too long, because they have water restrictions and Grandad takes them really seriously.'

Kate paused, presumably mentally checking off her list to make sure she hadn't forgotten anything forbidden.

'Grandad has a bit of a temper, and he loves to test people, but whatever happens, don't agree to anything that makes you feel uncomfortable.'

By now I was feeling thoroughly uncomfortable. To make matters worse, I felt every inch the city slicker. Tight black jeans, tattoos, soft hands, clean fingernails, a Harley Davidson shirt, no actual Harley Davidson. He was going to eat me alive.

'Are you sure you're okay?' asked Kate. I tried to smile. 'Don't worry too much, but whatever you do don't agree to drive anywhere with him.'

This wasn't really an issue – I didn't have my driver's licence. 'Definitely don't mention that,' added Kate. 'Grandad has been driving since he was five years old and he'll see it as a weakness.'

I sneezed again. Kate tensed as the ute rolled to a stop alongside us. A gnarled hand offered a thumbs up from the open window.

All I could think was: *don't get out of the car.*

* * * * * * *

The next few hours went better than we all could've hoped.

Ian seemed nice enough. Rough around the edges, sure, but in a salt of the earth kind of way. Like most old men, he kept a ballpoint pen in his top pocket and smelled faintly of Werther's Originals.

He was bemused by our selection of hire car. 'A Hyundai Getz, mate?' he laughed without smiling. 'Was everything else broken?' I made a mental note to never hire a Hyundai again, though I wasn't sure why.

Kate's grandmother Betty was more my speed. 'Give us a cuddle then,' she said by way of introduction, scooping me up into her bosom. Kate was forever boasting that her grandma gave the best hugs and it was hard to disagree.

In the evening we played cards, Ian and Betty pleasantly bickering for our entertainment. Each time he removed his false teeth for laughs she'd threaten to leave him. 'Not if I leave you first,' came the reply. They had lived this way for nearly sixty years, the rhythm of their delivery suggesting a well-rehearsed double act.

I stuck to the rules, closing the fridge quickly and showering for thirty seconds tops. When I eventually won a round of bridge, I could sense my stock was rising with Ian. 'Not bad, Soft Hands.'

'I think Grandad really likes you,' whispered Kate later that night. She was visiting me in my bedroom, which was actually a large linen closet full of sheets that hadn't been touched since the eighties. Perfect for my sneezing.

She spoke softly because we weren't supposed to be in the same room, another don't: men and women don't share a bed until they're married. I was pleased to be making progress and I didn't want Kate to ruin it for me now. She snuck out and I sneezed myself to sleep.

The next morning was the beginning of the worst day of my life.

Kate was feeling cocky. Ian had started using my real name instead of constantly calling me Soft Hands. I was content with these baby steps, but Kate wanted too much too soon: 'I want you to spend some proper time with Grandad.'

I pointed out that we *were* spending proper time together. Already that day I had watched him shoot a kangaroo and then bludgeon its joey to death. 'Bloody pests,' Ian had explained, hurling two generations of dead roo onto the back of his ute. 'Overpopulated and rooting nonstop.' What more could we squeeze into the day?

Our discussion was interrupted by the sweet smell of scones. While farm life wasn't for me – too quiet, too violent, too dusty – I could certainly get around the amount of snacking. Betty seemed to be baking at half-hour intervals.

As we sat to enjoy morning tea, I could sense Kate was about to be the unwitting architect of my demise. 'So maybe you'd like to help Grandad take the coolroom back into town?' she asked.

Not really, I thought, no. If anything, I would be a hindrance; I had no idea what the coolroom was, why it was headed back to town, or what might happen once we'd dropped it off.

But in my experience, male bonding typically stems from a made-up task that doesn't really require two people but is instead just an excuse for men to be alone together. And so my soft hand was forced.

'I'd love to, Ian.'

* * * * * * *

With the coolroom safely delivered into town – the purpose of this mission still a mystery to me – we settled into our drive back to the farm. I was struck by how much a man like Ian was perfectly suited to his surroundings.

Like the property he oversaw, Ian was a vast expanse. Sitting in the driver's seat he looked easily twice my size. The seatbelt pulled taut across his belly, enormous hands gripping the steering wheel, dust drifting off his shirt every time he changed gears. I desperately wanted to get a better look at his huge ears – they ran the entire length of the side of his head – but I was wary of Ian catching me staring.

Using the speed limit as more of a guideline, we flew through the front gate and headed for home. 'I just want to show you something,' said Ian, hooking a hard left.

We pulled up alongside a shed that looked to be on its last legs, and inside were a series of semi-trailers and trucks, parked neatly in a row – not a Hyundai to be seen. We walked the length of the shed and I got the distinct impression I was supposed to offer an opinion.

'Such big trucks.'

Ian was confused and who could blame him. He lumbered off towards a tractor, while my gaze drifted back towards the house. I imagined Betty fussing about the kitchen, dipping in and out of the fridge, gathering everything she needed to fix us some sandwiches. She had a habit of generously slathering butter on bread which I deeply appreciated, though my arteries did not.

The boom of instructions pulled me out of my snack reverie and into a terrifying reality – there was Ian, yelling at me from a tractor. 'Mate, I need to take this for a fix-up,' he said. 'Are you right to drive the ute back to the house? Just park her outside.'

And just like that, he was gone. Before I could even admit to the very thing I was told never to admit – I can't drive! – Ian tractored off into the distance.

The panic was real. Unsure what to do, I hopped into the ute, hoping that a hidden talent might emerge, like those people who awake from a coma speaking fluent French.

I scanned the backseat, looking for ... what? An instruction manual, a Dummies' Guide, a cyanide pill. No luck on any front, but there was a shotgun resting casually behind the passenger seat just to make the entire experience more intimidating. It felt very much like I was chauffeuring my own murder weapon.

In the distance, I could see the tractor slowing down and turning. Perhaps Ian had realised what he had done, or perhaps he was just curious to see what might happen next. Weren't we all?

While I was undeniably car-illiterate, I had forced my mother into a few stressful driving lessons when I first got my learner's permit. 'It's not for you, Thomas,' she had said, passive aggressively gripping the dashboard. 'And it's certainly not for me.'

But I must have retained something from our few trips because eventually muscle memory kicked in. I tried the key and gave it a little gas, but all it produced was a horrible gurgling sound. I continued this tactic, praying the car would catch flames and then I'd never have to explain myself.

The noise inside the ute was matched by another noise – the tractor starting up. Ian was heading back my way. Oh, dear. Suddenly, my entire future with Kate, my chance at happiness, depended on starting this fucking ute.

Turning to a foolproof method that had served me well in the past, I pulled my phone out. There is a YouTube tutorial for everything and if I could just ... no signal. No reception. Not a single bar.

Ian pulled up alongside me and I wound down the window. From the outside, it probably looked like two friendly neighbours stopping to exchange pleasantries.

'What the fuck is wrong with you?' barked Ian, breaking the illusion.

'You're stalling it. You need to release the clutch. Have you got it in the right gear, mate?'

All of the above meant very little to me, but by now I was sweating profusely and feeling increasingly nervous, so I resorted to diffusing in the best way I knew how. Seizing on one thing he said and pretending that was the problem all along. 'Oh, of course, the clutch,' I lied, looking around for where that might be.

Ian was off the tractor, making me all the more conscious of the gun in the back. He walked over to the ute, rested his forearms on the window and leant in, appearing for a second to look like a rural prostitute, before resuming his rant.

'You're crunching the gearbox! You're going to fuck my ute!'

All I wanted from this weekend was some polite country folk, a few homemade meals, possibly an open fire, topped off by the kind of thank you sex that comes with putting up with someone else's family. Instead, I was in a living nightmare being yelled at about a gearbox by a man I had known for less than forty-eight hours. 'Clutch, then brake, then gear, ya moron!' he screamed.

The increasing violence in Ian's voice seemed to spur something on in both the ute and me; miraculously we conjured up the right combination of foot, pedals and gear moves. The ute sprang to life once more.

'Fuckin' finally! Now kill the motor and wait for me, I'll lead the way,' instructed Ian.

Killing the motor was absolutely off the table. Getting this to start was a one-time deal and there was little chance of it happening ever again. This is it, Ian, strap in my friend. I'm driving now.

'You follow me back,' I yelled out the window, aware that this was the kind of statement I would pay for later.

Now that I had the old girl moving, I decided to give it a little, high on the thrill of watching the speedometer spike as I pushed my foot down.

If I had known then what I know now, I probably would've just kept driving, steering the ute through an open gate and onto the highway. *Never look back, Thomas, it's just you and the open road and a loaded shotgun.* But at the time, I figured it was best to do as I was told – mostly.

As I neared the house, I recalled that Ian had instructed me not to worry about parking inside the shed: 'Just leave her outside.'

Hoping to win him over, I decided to go above and beyond. I eased the ute perfectly into position inside the shed, triumphantly bringing my lead foot down on the brake.

I've always rolled my eyes when people describe things as 'happening in slow motion'. Surely everything happens in regular time and it's only when you replay it in your head that it seems to slow down? But as the ute lurched forward and I found myself sailing through the air, I finally understood what they meant. The back wall crumbled under the force of the crash and the ute came to a stop half-in, half-out.

At the time I had no idea what was happening, or why, though I would later learn I had committed a cardinal manual-drive sin. Braking without either pushing on the clutch or putting the vehicle into neutral causes it to jump forward, taking with it your hopes and dreams. Or in this case, the entire back wall of Ian's shed.

But I wasn't really focused on the *why* at this point, I was more worried about the *how*. As in 'how will Ian dispose of my corpse when this is over?'

Before I had the chance to finish that thought, there was another crash from above. An old rusted box had slid off a shelf, denting the bonnet of the car and cracking in half.

It looked to me like a medieval torture device, but on closer inspection it was clearly some kind of archaic drill. In years to come, it was revealed the drill was a family heirloom – odd choice of heirloom – and that by breaking it, I had in effect broken Ian's heart.

The falling of the drill had dislodged a barrel full of oil which toppled to the floor and burst open. Assuming the comedy of errors had come to a close, I forced my car door open and stepped onto the crime scene only to feel a painful twinge in my neck.

The crash had angered an old wasps' nest and now I was being stung repeatedly. Based on the intensity and ferocity it was, presumably, the queen. Welcome to my worst day.

Kate and Betty came running out to see what had happened. Betty was holding a tray of muffins, which was easily the most devastating part of the entire ordeal.

'Oh my god, what have you done?' yelled Kate. Unable to explain due to the wasp orgy I was hosting, I directed her attention to my neck. 'Grandma, get the methylated spirits!' she yelled, swatting away the wasps.

Betty returned with a meths-soaked tea towel and dabbed gently at the stings, ooh-ing and aah-ing as she worked. 'Hold this to your neck,' she said, placing an icepack in my hands. 'Cold compress, it'll help numb the pain.'

With water trickling down my back, I surveyed the damage. There was no getting around it, this was a situation. No one spoke.

Outside, I heard Ian kill the tractor engine, and wondered, quite seriously, if that would be the last thing he killed that afternoon. Rounding the corner, he took in the sight. Betty, who'd reclaimed the discarded muffins, Kate looking shocked, me icing my neck and wondering if my bee allergy would have a wasp crossover and what that might mean.

Then, in what remains one of the most distinct visuals of my life, Ian tossed his Akubra hat on the ground and stamped on it. Stamped it into the dirt. It was pure bush poetry, raw instinctual anger which would've been close to beautiful had I not been the sole cause of his rage.

He then unleashed a torrent of cursing that to this day I can recall at a moment's notice.

'No doubt in my mind,' Ian roared, 'you are an absolutely, rolled gold ... USELESS CUNT OF A MAN!'

This was Betty's cue to leave and I was relieved: neither she nor the muffins deserved to see this. Kate bravely stayed by my side, because that's what good partners and potential eyewitnesses must do.

The words continued to spew out, Ian frothing at the mouth. 'MY UTE, MY DRILL, MY SHED.' The verbal stocktake of all the things I'd ruined wasn't helping and by this point, he was really worked up. 'How could you be so stupid?' he said, pacing back and forth past his soiled hat. 'How did this happen?!'

He had asked the question so it felt like the right time to confess; the truth will set you free and all that.

'Ian, I don't actually have my driver's licence,' I explained. 'I can't even drive an automatic!'

A part of me hoped Ian would keel over laughing, the big reveal landing like a punchline to a joke he wasn't in on: *He can't even drive an automatic!* Cue applause.

Instead, it turns out the truth did not set me free, but it did set Ian off once more. Kate led me by the hand past her imploding grandfather and back into the house, where Betty and the muffins were waiting for us.

She suggested it might be a smart idea to go for a drive while Ian cooled down. 'Take a muffin for the road, won't you?' urged Betty, and I obliged.

* * * * * * *

Four years later and we turn off the road into the same long driveway. Not much has changed; drought has muted some of the colours on the property, but otherwise, it's all still here: the dirt, the dust, the quiet.

There is one difference though: this time, I'm driving. I navigate the Hyundai Getz (an automatic) over the bumps as Kate sits in the passenger seat, unsuspecting. In my pocket is a ring, and I'm rehearsing the words in my head.

In the years since the Crash it's become a beloved part of family folklore. Each Christmas someone drunkenly slurs 'remember when?' which always ends with Ian and me offering up our differing versions.

When Ian got wind of my plan to propose it was his idea that I do it on the farm, Kate's favourite place. The property was sold a couple of years ago, but Ian called the new owner and let him know I'd be coming out for a visit. 'I told him not to shoot if he sees some strange fella knocking about,' he laughed. How far we've come.

We drive past the shed where the big trucks once lived and we both turn to look.

I put the car in park and this time it doesn't move. For a second everything is still. The sun sets, slow and deliberate, like it only does in the country. Kate gets out, walks the familiar ground and smiles at me. This will be the best day of my life.

THE F*** UP HALL OF FAME

Rotten Apple

> **Name**: Ronald Wayne   **Rating**: 10/10
>
> **Fuck-up**: In 1976, the Apple co-founder sold his ten per cent stake in the fledgling company.

In terms of costly mistakes, they don't come much bigger than the one Ronald Wayne made back in 1976.

While working for the computer company Atari, Ronald met a couple of young whippersnappers by the names of Steve Jobs and Steve Wozniak.

The two Steves were smart and canny technicians, both in their twenties, with grand plans to rule the world. However, their youthful exuberance was matched only by their youthful stubbornness, and more often than not the pair ended up butting heads.

Desperate for a calming presence, they tapped Ronald on the shoulder and asked if he would help them with their decision-making. Ronald agreed, inviting both parties to his house for a two-hour meeting.

The result of that meeting was the birth of a little side hustle called Apple Inc.

The company was officially formed on 1 April 1976, with ownership split three ways: Jobs and Wozniak each took a 45 per cent share of the business and Wayne received 10 per cent so that he could act as a deciding vote in future disagreements. Ronald himself drew up the contract, signed by all three co-founders.

Twelve days later Ronald sold his ten per cent stake back to his co-founders for a measly US$800. Today that stock is worth an estimated AUD$96,000,000,000. That's nine zeros for those counting, as in ninety-six BILLION dollars.

So did Ronald figure Apple was rotten to the core and decide to cut ties? Not exactly.

The Apple co-founder has gone on the record to explain that while he was certain the two Steves would be successful: 'I didn't know when . . . or how long it would take to achieve that success.'

It's also been reported that Ronald was worried about the risks that come with getting in on the ground floor of an untested venture, fearing that if Apple went belly up, he would be on the hook for 10 per cent of their debts.

Of course, Apple didn't go belly up. Instead it became the most influential tech company of all time, a worldwide symbol of innovation and invention.

In Ronald's defence, he has always maintained that leaving Apple after just twelve days was the right decision, otherwise he might have 'wound up the richest man in the cemetery'.

From the outside looking in, however, missing out on a billion-dollar windfall is undeniably hard to stomach.

To make matters worse, in the early 1990s Ronald sold the original contract for just US$500. In 2011, the historic document fetched US$1.6 million at auction.

Feel better now?

We May Need to Amputate

Adam's story

Now look, before we get into this, there are a couple of things you should probably know about me.

I'm not big on dating; it's not really my thing, you know? I met my first girlfriend at seventeen and was with her for eight years. We broke up and straight after that I fell into another eight-year relationship. Copy and paste.

I'd always been a relationship guy or, as my last girl called me during our break-up chat, 'a serial monogamist'.

'You're a serial monogamist, Adam,' she said, patting my hand softly and shaking her head. *Hold up, isn't that the whole point?* 'You need to get out there, explore the world, meet new people.'

So when I found myself single at thirty-three, that's exactly what I did. I explored the world; I got out there. I met new people. One of them was Adriana. We connected on a dating app but at first I was convinced Adriana was a Russian bot. She was all bee-stung lips and computer-generated curves. It was too much.

'There's no way a girl who looks like that isn't about to fleece you,' joked my friend Arka, handing back my phone. I'd barely been on the dating app for a week and here was this 10-out-of-10 asking about my weekend.

'Adam, you're not a bad-looking guy, but you and I don't date people named Adriana. We end up with Jennys or Amys, maybe a Simone. All I'm saying is if she seems too good to be true . . .' He trailed off.

It was flawed logic, but for some reason it worked, so with Arka's words of 'wisdom' – I use that term loosely – ringing in my ears I backed off, and yet she persisted.

Whenever I opened the app, there she was again with a cute message designed to pull me back in: videos of baby giraffes learning to stand or deaf people hearing for the first time. That's emotional shit. How do you ignore that?

We kept talking, but I kept waiting. Waiting for Adriana to show her hand and ask for my bank account details or a lump sum. After two weeks, it seemed like the moment had finally arrived, a message blinking in my inbox.

Hey I wanted to ask you something. The text cut off, but I was sure the next bit would read: *cAn u TraNsfeR me $10,000 biG boi?*

I opened the message, and my concern was immediately replaced by embarrassment, then delight: *Adam, is there a reason you haven't asked me out yet?*

Over the next month, Adriana and I went out a lot. Initially I was just excited she existed – take that, Arka! – but it quickly snowballed into more. By our fourth date, I could feel myself falling into old traps, the serial monogamist in me already planning our break-up in eight years' time.

Wary of making familiar mistakes, I decided to play it cool. Take it slow. That went out the window the night Adriana invited me back to her place during dinner. 'How do you feel about a sleepover?' she asked, grinning over her wine glass.

Adriana lived on the third floor of a smart apartment block, one of those buildings people would describe as 'having character'. I was back sleeping in my childhood bedroom at my parents' house, so anywhere that wasn't there had character to me.

'Now, I should warn you –' said Adriana, breaking off as she turned the key in the lock. (By this point I was so invested she could've admitted to having several bodies inside the apartment and I would've just stepped over them.) '– I have a cat, Mr Klaus, Klaus for short, and he can be a little protective.'

Like most normal people, I hate cats; they can't be trusted and always seem to be plotting. But I'd already spied Adriana's phone background – a picture of her cat – and stalked her Instagram, which was full of cat snaps and cat memes.

I even knew Mr Klaus had his own Instagram account, *@rebelwithoutaklaus*.

Bottom line: Adriana was a cat lady, which meant I was going to pretend to be a cat guy.

'Are you kidding? I love cats!'

Once inside the apartment, I went full pet-lover. It was still early days, and I wanted Adriana to know that whatever was important to her was important to me. That included Mr Klaus.

'Are you going to play with him all night?' asked Adriana, returning to the lounge room in considerably fewer layers than she had on before. Thank you, Mr Klaus.

* * * * * * *

The morning after you seal the deal with someone you genuinely like is a special kind of bliss. You've come through the build-up and now you're both giddy off the high of having finally done it.

As Adriana lay next to me scrolling through her phone, I could feel myself smiling and thinking, *I'd do anything for this girl.*

That was the moment the universe decided to call my bluff.

'Shit, my work needs me to go to New Zealand for the weekend,' said Adriana, her phone coming alive in a flurry of beeps.

She was the head of Asia-Pacific for a marketing and communications company and was always ducking off to take important-sounding calls. I was a jobbing actor who mainly received calls from my mum or the Tax Office.

'No, no, no! They need me to go tonight, oh, that's so annoying!'

As if forcing his way into the equation, Mr Klaus jumped on the bed and did that weird slinking body thing cats do, stretching his spine out. It made me feel uncomfortable.

'Are you going to miss me? Will you miss Mummy?' sang Adriana as she hauled a suitcase down from her wardrobe. I ignored the temptation to answer, figuring the question was directed at Mr Klaus.

Speaking of the cat, this was the perfect opportunity to double down and really show Adriana why we should be together forever, or at least the next eight years. A noble steed, stepping up in an hour of need.

'Hey, who is going to look after this little guy?' I asked, forcing myself to pat Mr Klaus.

'If you need someone, I can do it. I just live around the corner.'

To her credit, Adriana shot me down instantly. 'No, no, I can't ask you to do that, oh my god, you're so sweet though! I actually have someone lined up, I go away all the time, so a friend pops over, but thanks so much! Ohhh, you're so sweet!'

Fantastic. I'd done the right thing by offering but avoided the burden of responsibility. That's win-win territory.

Aware that Adriana needed to panic-pack for her work trip, I kissed her goodbye and bailed.

'Dinner when I get back?' she yelled from the bedroom as I headed for the door. 'Maybe you could come here, and I can cook?' Even better.

Later that afternoon, I missed a call from Adriana. She must've been close to checking into her flight, which meant she was ringing me from the airport. That's a big deal, you only call someone from the airport if you really like them, so I was feeling pretty chuffed as I hit redial.

'Was just thinking –' I began, when Adriana cut me off. She sounded panicked.

'Adam, I'm so sorry, I hate to do this, but the friend I lined up to look after Klaus has just pulled out. Is there any chance you could still do it?'

Heavy breathing, and the echo of flights being called in the background. 'Of course I can, Adriana.'

After offering a thousand thank-yous, Adriana explained that the key was under the mat and all I had to do was feed him and clean the litter.

'And do you mind hanging out with him a little bit? He gets lonely.'

Absolutely, no sweat.

* * * * * * *

The day after my first glorious visit, I returned to Adriana's apartment. The key was under the mat, just as she promised, and I offered a sing-songy greeting as I entered. 'Hey, little buddy!'

Mr Klaus was sitting in the middle of an armchair like he'd been expecting me. I hadn't noticed his soulless black eyes when we last met, but now that they were tracking my every move, they were hard to ignore.

'There you are, just sitting patiently, that's not at all terrifying.' I tried my best to sound casual; he wasn't buying it. 'So, what's been happening?' Mr Klaus remained silent, though I was sure even if he could talk, he wouldn't share his secrets.

Adriana had followed up her airport phone call with a text leaving detailed instructions on the cat's many needs.

He loves a cuddle in the afternoon, and his favourite food is Whiskas – there's a can in the kitchen. Half when you arrive, half when you leave. And he's such a joker! He loves his fishing line toy so give that a go! Don't worry about staying too long, an hour should do it! Thanks again, lifesaver! xx

An hour! That's a hard pass from me. I was staying fifteen minutes; twenty tops. I skipped the cuddle, gave Mr Klaus half his food, then settled in for the fishing line game Adriana had talked up.

It involved a plastic fish attached to the end of a fishing rod. Klaus was supposed to jump back and forth trying to catch the fish. Instead, he just sat there looking bored.

'Well, that was fun,' I said after a fruitless ten minutes. 'Why don't we send Mum a pic so that I can get out of here?'

Having grown up with a mother who was determined to capture every moment of our upbringing, I'd been well-schooled in the art of rustling up a smile for the sake of a happy snap.

'Come on, kids, everybody in,' she would say, gripping my brother, sister and me by the shoulders and squeezing us. 'Big smiles please, and one, two, three!'

I used this same tactic on Klaus, wrestling him into a photo and firing it through to Adriana. The reply came back within minutes. *OMG! My boys. I miss you both so much!*

she wrote, followed by a photo of her fake-frowning. *Send me some more!*

I rushed through the remainder of our afternoon, documenting it all for Adriana's benefit. Here's Mr Klaus eating the rest of his foul-smelling cat food. Here's Mr Klaus scowling out the window at local children. And finally, here's Mr Klaus licking his anus.

These are soooooooo cute, gushed Adriana. *Adam, you are my hero, thank you so much!*

With hero status achieved and welcome-home sex almost guaranteed, it was time to bounce.

By now, Klaus had started sulking near the front door, clearly hoping Adriana would return and disappointed she hadn't. I felt his pain but also wanted to get home ASAP. Mum had made schnitzel, and if I didn't get in quick Dad would polish off the lot.

I picked Klaus up with one hand, and deposited him safely back on the couch, remembering to grab the empty tin of cat food from the kitchen so it didn't stink out the joint. I gave the apartment one last scan, making sure nothing was out of place, then headed for the door.

Now, I hate to play the blame game in regard to what happened next but let me just go on record as saying I exclusively blame the people who designed the door to Adriana's apartment.

She'd already flagged that Klaus loved to escape and that he was very fast, a bad combo for any potential pet sitter. 'Please, please, please,' she'd warned. 'Be extra careful when coming and going.'

My carefully considered exit plan had been to back my body up against the door, crack it an inch, and slide through silently. One thing I hadn't allowed for, however, was the five hundred locks on the door, each requiring two hands to operate. Sure, the place had character; it also had intense security.

Back on the couch, Klaus was busy licking himself, so I figured I was in the clear. After conquering the multiple deadbolts, I opened the door. One sniff of the outside world and it was over. The furry fucker slipped through my legs and shot out like an arrow. Klaus was gone.

The immediate horror was immense, a highlight reel of worst-case scenarios flashed across my brain. Mr Klaus lying motionless in the middle of the road, Adriana crying on the phone to me from New Zealand: 'I trusted you, Adam,' she'd sob brokenly. 'You said you loved cats!'

I remembered I had the empty tin of food which I could use to lure him out from wherever he was hiding, but I would have to do it quietly. Adriana's place was bookended by apartments. The last thing I wanted to do was raise the alarm and then have to explain to her neighbours – who I'd never met – why I was creeping around their building with a can of Whiskas.

My only option was to whisper-yell for the cat, while trying to keep an eye on any sudden movements. 'Misssterrr Klausssssss, little buddy?' Nothing. 'Where are you, Mr Klaussssss?'

I ran down the stairs, taking two at a time, reaching the ground floor. In the darkness, two devil eyes glared back at me from underneath the staircase. Sweet relief: Mr Klaus was in the building.

'Never thought I'd be so happy to see you, little buddy!' He hissed back in reply, letting me know the feeling was far from mutual. Desperate to coax him out, I started tapping the empty food tin on the stairs while calling his name. I'm giving it my all at this point. Neighbours be damned.

'Klausssss,' I quivered, my voice scaling several octaves. 'Hey buddddddy, hey Klaussss.' He hissed back, and I went again, 'Heyyyyy Klausssss.'

Eventually, he softened, wooed by the scent of the Whiskas, and as he came towards me, I congratulated myself on this stroke of genius. Klaus had been rescued, Adriana would be none the wiser, and we'd live happily ever after. How wrong I was to trust the untrustworthy.

I bent down to pick him up, and that was when Klaus launched himself at me, sinking his claws deep into my right hand. He scratched and swiped, a manic look in his crazy cat eyes as he ripped into the flesh.

A wicked gash opened up near my thumb, and the gushing blood sent my stomach spinning. My gut instinct was to pile drive this motherfucking meower into the ground and just tell Adriana he escaped: 'Hey, I'm so sorry Klaus ran away, and in unrelated news, I got my arm caught in a meat tenderiser!'

But then I had a vision of her angelic face, tears welling as I broke the news. 'Don't cry, beautiful creature,' I would say, wiping her tears with my mangled hand. 'I bet Klaus is somewhere out there living his best life!'

Tempting as that was, I knew Adriana would never forgive me if I accidentally-on-purpose murdered her pet. Using the adrenaline coursing through my veins, I sprinted back up the two flights of stairs, Klaus still attached to my hand.

We made it to the apartment, and he finally let go, scurrying out of sight. My only thought was to get out of there, so I opened another tin of food to keep Klaus happy and left. As I walked away, I noticed a smear of red on Adriana's front door. Blood.

The mind ticked over: if Adriana's neighbours see the door, they're going to assume a violent homicide has taken place. To make matters worse, the cat assault has made it hard to keep a low profile, so it's also safe to assume that someone might have seen me.

Basically, if I wanted to keep this ordeal under wraps then cleaning up the blood was non-negotiable.

Obviously, going back inside was a death sentence, so I tried spitting on my non-wounded hand to clean it up. This only served to smoosh and spread the blood, so that the door resembled either a) an expensive abstract artwork or b) the macabre drawing of a young child.

Either way, it looked terrible, and now I had backed myself into a bloody corner. My best bet? To fetch something from the kitchen and clean the mess.

If I could run this scenario back, I would've just gone home, told Adriana the truth and ordered her a replacement, blood-free door. Instead, I re-entered the cauldron of pain, tiptoed to the kitchen, grabbed some paper towel and tiptoed back.

Just as I approached the door and its many, many locks, I heard the tingle of a bell, one of Klaus's toys. I turned in the direction of the noise, but Klaus wasn't there. That's because he was underneath me.

Before I could even reach for the doorknob, Klaus launched again. He'd returned to finish the job, digging his claws *back into my original wounds*.

At this point, I was about to black out with pain, so any consideration of Adriana's feelings flew out the window.

I sent Klaus hurtling across the room and slammed the door shut. Attacked by the same cat twice in one night.

I staggered back to my car and collapsed into the driver's seat. The only thing that stopped me passing out was the beep of my phone. One new message from Adriana: *Everything okay in the end?*

My bleeding fingers punched out a response. *All good.*

* * * * * * *

You ever hear those stories about people who survive super traumatic episodes through sheer force of will? They'll be in a head-on car crash and then walk like ten kilometres on a broken leg to the nearest town and it's only later on when someone asks, 'Hey, how the hell did you get so far on your messed up leg?' that they'll suddenly pass out from the pain. It's like your body blocks it out until someone else reminds you. You know stories like that? That's how my drive home felt.

I remember looking at my hand resting on the steering wheel and thinking: *it's not so bad. Okay, there's a dull pain vibrating in my right arm, but nothing a couple of Panadol won't fix.*

It wasn't until I walked through the door and saw the colour drain out of Mum's face that the pain came thundering back. 'Michael, come quick, I think Adam might need stitches!' she yelled, putting the schnitzel back in the oven and guiding me to the lounge room.

My dad is pretty old-school in his approach to anything pain-related: A laconic 'You'll be right' greeted anything from a grazed knee to a broken arm when we were kids.

So imagine my alarm when the old man took one look at my pulverised hand and reeled back in horror. 'Christ almighty, that definitely needs stitches, mate.' He leant in for a closer look, gently turning my arm to better survey the damage. 'Christ,' he repeated to himself.

'I don't feel like going to the hospital,' I said.

Dad's face lit up: he frothed on a home remedy. 'Suze, fetch the Tarzan's Grip, will ya?'

For those unaware, there are medical-grade super glues you can use to seal wounds shut; Tarzan's Grip is not one of them. 'Isn't that for around the house?' said Mum, the frantic sound of drawers opening and closing in the background.

'He'll be right,' replied Dad, predictable as ever. By the time we tracked down the Tarzan's Grip, Dad's confidence was wavering. I believe his exact words were: 'If you're up for it, I'm up for it.'

This hardly instilled a lot of faith, but I was borderline delirious, so my decision-making was cooked. Go on Dad, whack a bit of Tarzan's Grip on, and let's see what happens!

Miraculously, it kind of worked. I held the wound shut,

Dad applied the glue, and when I let go ten minutes later, the skin was joined. 'Ta-da! Thank me later,' he joked, walking back into the lounge room with a spring in his step. 'And try to get some rest.'

I went to bed cautiously optimistic, before waking up early in the grip of a white-hot pain so brutal I wouldn't inflict it on my worst enemy, except maybe Klaus. My whole body was on fire and the hand had tripled in size.

'Mum, Dad, I think something is wrong,' I said, switching on their bedroom light and thrusting the offending hand in front of them. I could tell from Dad's face I looked in a bad way: he was shitting bricks.

'Glue might've been a bad idea,' he said, pulling on a shirt and keeping his eyes on my novelty-sized hand. 'We might need to duck down to the hospital.' *You reckon?*

As we bustled through the Emergency doors, Dad was still in damage control, doing his best to convince me it was all going to be okay.

'Who could've known that it would turn out this way,' he muttered, as I drifted in and out of consciousness. 'They'll probably just give you some anti-inflams, something for the swelling, ya know?'

The last thing I recall before hitting the deck was a concerned-looking doctor examining my hand and signalling to his colleague behind the counter. 'Call a specialist. Now!'

* * * * * * *

I woke up in the dead of night with my hand raised in the air like I'd fallen asleep waiting to ask a question.

It turned out I was in a gallows sling, which is even more uncomfortable than it sounds. You sleep like that so the blood rushes out of your hand and forces the swelling down.

I knew nothing of this at the time. In fact, I'd have barely known where I was if not for the stench of hospital-grade disinfectant and the methodic beeping. Suddenly it all flooded back: the fainting, the panic, the call for a specialist.

The beeping came from a nearby bed. The curtains were drawn, but I could see two pairs of shoes crowded around the bed frame. Whoever they were talking about sounded rough, like they were breathing underwater.

'There must be something you can do,' said one set of shoes. 'Can't you take him to the ICU? What about a transfusion?'

The other set of shoes shuffled on the spot. 'I'm really, truly sorry, but you're going to have to come to terms with the stage he's at. He's not got long left. Perhaps you'd like to make some calls? If it helps, he's not in any pain.'

As if proving a point, the person in the bed let out a low guttural gurgle that sounded painful.

Not long after, the first set of shoes started her grim ring around, and within an hour, the room was buzzing with people. I listened to them weep before finally tripping into a fitful sleep around three o'clock.

The following morning two surgeons walked into my room. First came a slow-moving man who looked about a thousand years old, backed up by a stern lady with a severe haircut.

The mourners were nowhere to be seen; the bed next to me now empty.

Having barely slept, I felt a little groggy, but I started to pay attention when the stern lady began using words like 'necrosis', 'bacterial infection' and 'gangrenous'. And you can bet your bottom dollar I was wide awake when the ancient one straightened up and said: 'We may need to amputate.'

All right, so just to take stock. Everything in my life was golden until I offered to pet sit for a girl I barely knew. After being mauled by her cat, which has a stupid name, I'm now being told I may lose a hand. As my dad would say, 'she'll be right'.

Speaking of Dad, he entered the room just as my emergency surgery was locked in for that morning. 'We'll do everything we can,' said the stern lady, but it felt like an empty promise.

An hour later, I was flat on the operating table, cursing Klaus as the drugs took over.

* * * * * * *

Waking up expecting to have one hand and realising you still have two is a joy I can't recommend highly enough. If you ever get the chance to almost have your hand amputated, grab it. With both hands.

'The good news is we were able to save the hand,' explained the ancient doc. 'The bad news is the surgery will leave a pretty nasty scar.' And he wasn't wrong! To this day, my right hand bears the mark of the beast: a giant scar in the shape of the letter C.

C for cat.

Following the success of the surgery, they kept me in hospital for another three days, and then I had to do six months of daily rehab to regain full use of my hand. It's still not back to normal – I can't do push-ups or open jar lids – but at least I have both hands. I can still clap.

Adriana was super apologetic about the whole ordeal, and we kept seeing each other for a little bit, maybe a couple of months, but it became too weird. Every time we hung out, or held hands, it hovered in the air between us. When we broke up, Klaus unfollowed me on Instagram.

I've just started seeing someone new, and it's going well. She's more of a dog person.

THE F*** UP HALL OF FAME

The Unluckiest Man in the Luckiest Village

Name: Costis Mitsotakis   **Rating**: 8/10

Fuck-up: An entire village goes all-in on Spain's richest lottery. When they win the jackpot, everyone shares the spoils – except for Costis, who forgot to buy a ticket.

There's nothing worse than feeling like the odd one out, especially when that feeling costs you a life-changing payday. It's a tough pill to swallow – just ask Costis Mitsotakis.

In 2011, Costis was living in the Spanish village of Sodeto, population 250. The Greek filmmaker had moved to Sodeto for love, but the relationship fell apart. Costis now spent his days nursing a broken heart while working the land on a small farm, tucked away on the outskirts of town.

December rolled around, and there was a buzz in the air, it was time for *El Gordo*. This is the grand prize of Spain's annual Christmas lottery. Held three days before Christmas, *El Gordo* has the dual honour of being the world's second-oldest lottery, while being considered the richest jackpot.

The English translation of *El Gordo* is 'The Fat One', which seems pretty fitting for Costis's tale, because as far as fuck-ups are concerned, this is the fattest of the lot.

Each year the Housewives' Association in Sodeto pool their money and go all-in, pinning the town's hopes on a single number. They then go door-to-door selling shares in that number, earning a percentage of each sale. In 2011 their lucky number was 58,268.

Despite tough economic conditions that year, everyone in town bought at least one ticket – everyone, that is, but Costis. The Housewives' Association didn't make it as far as his farm, and Costis didn't follow up: *El Gordo* is a Spanish tradition, and as a foreigner he was out of the loop.

On 22 December, eyes were glued to television sets around the country as the winning number was announced: 58,268 – the exact number on the 1800 tickets sold in Sodeto. Against the odds, the town had hit the *El Gordo* jackpot, sharing in a pool of €740 million (AUD $1.2 billion).

Every single Sodeto resident was rich in an instant, from struggling farmers to humble shopkeepers. Depending on how many tickets they'd bought, villagers pocketed hundreds of thousands of Euros; some made millions.

Adding insult to injury, even Costis's ex-girlfriend had a ticket! But the Greek filmmaker was the odd one out, left with nothing. Well, almost nothing.

When the news broke, the people of Sodeto assembled in the town centre to celebrate. Despite his disappointment, Costis went along to the celebrations and started filming, the unluckiest man in the luckiest town capturing everything around him.

Eventually, Costis turned his misfortune into a documentary, *Cuando Tocó* (*When Touched*). The film tells the story of Sodeto's incredible luck, and how the town fared in the aftermath of such a tremendous win.

While Costis maintains to this day that he doesn't regret missing out, he's purchased a ticket in The Fat One every year since.

We Are Family

Steph's story

Ask any woman in the world, and she'll tell you straight: there is nothing sexier than watching your boyfriend make a good first impression on the family.

Josh was a total natural, bantering with the blokes and charming the ladies. All afternoon he'd buzzed around the backyard effortlessly: offering drinks, cracking gags – like he'd always been there.

'Anyone for some sauv blanc?' he'd ask, filling our glasses to the brim and causing a serious tingle between my thighs.

We were twenty-one and in love, that blissful period when small gestures feel big, and something as simple as a generous pour makes you desperate to be alone together.

Josh and I had flown to Sydney from Geelong for a family reunion that doubled as a housewarming party. My Aunt Kate had recently bought a gorgeous property in the Southern Highlands. The place was huge: something like seven bedrooms and eight bathrooms.

'The whole family can crash, there's plenty of room,' Aunt Kate said when she called to extend the invite. 'Bring your new fella, too. He's more than welcome.'

Poor Josh, talk about the deep end. We'd been serious for about six months and while I had planned to bring him to Sydney eventually, I was picturing a quiet weekend with a few key people, maybe a couple of cousins. Ease him into the set-up slowly.

Instead, here we were, the full Fitzgerald family experience.

Aunts, uncles, cousins, kids – even my grandmother had travelled solo from the mid-North Coast by train, never missing an opportunity to get amongst a good party.

To his credit, Josh hadn't blinked when I suggested crashing the get-together. 'Let's rip the bandaid off,' he laughed. 'If I'm going to meet one, I may as well meet 'em all.'

He even met Uncle Ron, who I wasn't actually related to but who'd been around for as long as I could remember. Not to mention all Aunt Kate's friends and neighbours she'd gone ahead and invited. A melting pot of strange faces, small talk and introductions. Welcome to the family, Josh.

Like all our catch-ups this one had started civilised and descended into chaos. Wherever you looked, there were demolished cheese boards, half-moons of brie that had been hacked away at all afternoon. Kids zipped in and out of the backyard, bumping into each other and bruising their knees. Eventually, you'd find them zonked in different corners of the house, sleeping wherever they fell.

As it got dark, the oldies really started to cut loose. Last time I checked Aunt Kate was blending margaritas, a dead giveaway that things were about to lift off.

In the backyard, my brother Darren and Uncle Ron had Josh cornered by the barbecue. Josh was talking and my brother was buckled over laughing. Even Uncle Ron, who was a tough nut to crack, seemed to be enjoying Josh's story.

Damn. The more he fitted in, the more I craved him.

'Josh, can I borrow you for a minute?' I said, interrupting the love-in. My brother gave me a nod which I knew meant 'good bloke'.

'Everything okay?' asked Josh, taking me by the hand. 'I think this is all going really well.'

'It's going *so* well, which is exactly why I want you to myself,' I whispered mischievously. Josh quickly caught on. 'I'm done sharing now.'

As I led Josh down the side of the house, I heard Aunt Kate belting out Sister Sledge's 'We Are Family'.

Brilliant, I thought, the margaritas must've kicked in.

* * * * * * *

Sitting on the front verandah, I wasted no time in having a little fun of my own, kissing Josh with the fervent passion of new(ish) lovers.

'I've missed you all afternoon,' I purred, sliding my hand inside his shirt.

We were bang in the middle of the sweet spot: together less than a year, but we both knew it was serious, so every kiss felt electric. Sprinkle in Josh's impressive performance with my family, and I couldn't stop myself.

Hands and lips moving, brain ignoring the close-but-distant hum of people in the backyard.

'Steph, aren't you worried about –' Josh flicked his head back towards the house.

'I am, but also –' I kissed his neck, mmm, I'm a sucker for a nice neck, '– I want you.'

'I want you too,' Josh admitted, swinging me up onto his lap. He may have had reasonable self-control, but he was still a twenty-one-year-old guy, and the slightest whiff of interest was enough.

'Is there anywhere else we can go?' he asked, his curious hands working their way inside my shirt and up my back. With so many people sleeping over spare rooms were hard to come by and we'd wound up bunking with my younger cousin, Kimberley.

Out the back, I could hear Uncle Geoff kicking off a rendition of 'Let It Be' by the Beatles. He could hold a tune, and I knew my aunts would demand a couple of encores at least, which gave us a clear, though brief, window. Hopping off Josh's lap, I quietly opened the front door.

'Follow me,' I instructed, leading Josh inside.

The master bedroom was at the very front of the house, the furthest point possible from all the action in the backyard.

'We should be safe here but don't turn the light on,' I said, pushing Josh onto the bed, in the dim light I could make out his shape landing awkwardly.

'Wait, the coats,' he whispered, scrambling up again.

I remembered Aunt Kate had told everyone to leave their jackets and bags on the bed in the front room when we first arrived. The bed seemed to be piled high.

'Looks like we're just going to have to improvise,' I told Josh, reaching for his belt and unbuckling it.

'This is not how I saw the family reunion going,' he laughed, lifting my dress over my head.

'Glad you came?' I asked, peeling his shirt off. Josh gazed back at me, a cheeky grin on his face.

'I will be when you do,' he replied, nuzzling into my neck and spinning me round.

Avoiding coat mountain, I leant on the bed, while Josh remained standing, opting for a quick and effective position – summing up exactly what we were there to achieve and the timeframe we had to achieve it.

There's something strange about having sex in the dark; it forces you to be more aware of every move, every sensation. I could feel Josh behind me, I could feel my palms on the bed, but in the dark, it all melted away.

'You feel amazing,' murmured Josh, his hands on my hips.

I was lost in the blur, but I needed to hear him. 'Say my name.'

'You feel amazing, *Steph*.'

'Louder!'

'Steph, YOU FEEL AMAZING!'

One thing guaranteed to pull you right out of this magic is the booming sound of your aunt's voice, giving a tour of the house to her guests.

'And this up here is the master bedroom,' began Aunt Kate, followed by the terrifying rattle of a doorknob.

'Oh god!' whispered Josh as light flooded the room. We both froze.

'You'll notice it has the same high ceilings as the rest of the –'

I twisted round and locked eyes with Aunt Kate, who'd fallen silent, her mouth open. She was less than a metre and a half away from us, but because everyone was behind her, she managed to stop them from coming in.

'Um, actually ... why don't I show you the cellar next, that's always a big hit with guests,' said Kate, backing away in silent ecstasy. The look on her face told me she'd be dining out on this forever.

Aunt Kate switched the light off, closed the door, and we collapsed onto the bed.

'Ho-ly sh-it, Steph!' spluttered Josh, quickly pulling his pants up from around his ankles. He was freaking. 'Oh, god, your aunt saw everything! My ass right in her face, and you were bent over, and it was all just ... there.'

The image of Josh's bare ass flashed across my mind and I stifled a snort.

'Why are you laughing?'

'I'm sorry, I'm sorry,' I said to Josh, grabbing him by the waist before he could finish dressing. 'Why are you getting dressed?'

'Um ... because your aunt who I met for the first time tonight just busted me having sex with her niece, *in her brand-new house.*'

He tried to pull away, but I'd hooked my thumbs in the belt loops of his pants. He wasn't going anywhere.

'Josh, of all the people to interrupt, Aunt Kate is the best option,' I explained, resting my head against his stomach. 'No doubt she'll find it hilarious and tell the whole family and all her friends and everyone she's ever met, but trust me: right now, we're safer in here than we are out there.'

I sealed this comment with a kiss, pulling his face down to mine and bringing him in. We'd come this far there, no way was I throwing in the towel.

After a few minutes of working ourselves up, I thought the guilt had got to him again.

'Steph,' whispered Josh, he sounded something: scared, worried? No: cold.

'It's freezing, reckon we can get under the covers?'

* * * * * * *

Preparing myself for a blizzard of attention the minute we re-joined the party, as we got dressed I briefed Josh on what to expect.

'Sarcastic applause, maybe a little wolf-whistling.' He looked mortified. 'There's also a good chance Aunt Kate has told Mum.'

'Oh god! Your mum?' whispered Josh, pacing back and forth, 'This is bad.'

We'll soon find out, I thought, leading Josh out of the bedroom. At the very least, I figured Aunt Kate might be waiting for us at the end of the hall, demanding all the dirty details.

But as we walked back into the party, nothing seemed to have changed. My brother and Uncle Ron were arguing over who cooks a better steak on the barbecue, snoozing kids were piled up in the living room, the Fitzgerald sing-along was louder than ever. We slipped back outside, and Josh ducked off to the esky to grab us a couple of drinks.

It was then I finally spied Aunt Kate: she was mid-conversation, but we locked eyes – for the second time that night. *Here comes the public announcement*, I thought. *Brace yourself, Steph.*

Instead, she took a long sip from her margarita and winked. A kind of 'good on you' wink.

And that was that. No one else seemed to know a thing.

****

Sandra's story

A migraine pill and a lie-down was the advice my doctor had given me. The moment you feel a migraine coming on, she'd said, take one Naramig and lie down.

It had been a long afternoon; a lovely one, but a long one. It's wonderful seeing family but catching up can take it out of you, so I wasn't surprised when the migraine arrived. First came the pulsating in my head, then the blurry vision. The thumping music wasn't helping matters but try telling that to my sister Kate.

'Any chance we could turn it down a little?' I'd asked, knowing that the chances were slim-to-none. I was perched on the edge of the lounge, my legs crossed, Kate dancing around the coffee table. That quite adequately summed us up.

'Come on, sis!' yelled Kate, trying to pull me up to her makeshift dance floor. 'Have another drink, that'll sort your head, want me to fix you a marg?'

No, another drink wasn't the answer. I'd tried that a few times in the past, and it never worked, just made things worse. All I could do, should do, was take one Naramig and have a lie-down, just like the doctor said.

I excused myself and snuck off: better not to make a fuss, otherwise Kate would be on my case. We were complete opposites: Kate was older, but everyone picked her as younger. She was a little more fun than me, I suppose, a little more carefree. It certainly felt that way as I searched for a quiet corner while she danced up a storm.

The migraine was stronger now, pounding in time with

the music, and the nausea was borderline unbearable. I must find somewhere soon.

Staggering down the hallway, I recalled that Kate's bedroom was at the very front of the house, far away from the music. Earlier that evening I'd left my coat in there and remembered seeing a chaise longue on the far side of the bed, against the wall.

I planned to rest on the chaise for a moment, at least until the Naramig kicked in.

Leaving the light off – migraine sufferers will know that light sensitivity is one of the more testing symptoms – I groped my way through the dark, eventually finding the chaise and lying down.

Shutting my eyes, I willed the migraine away; willed sleep to take over. From deep in the house, I could make out a muffled argument over which song to play next. No doubt it would be a song Kate loved; one the family knew every word to.

I heard my brother Geoff's voice and then the sound of the piano. I loved it when he played. Thankfully, mercifully, with the sound of the piano, sleep washed over me.

I awoke sometime later: maybe five minutes, maybe an hour – it can be hard to gauge with a migraine – to the creak of the bedroom door. Even in my groggy state, I sensed two people enter the room, two sets of feet softly shuffling.

Figuring they'd come to collect their coats I remained still. The position of the chaise meant I was bathed in darkness so I was confident they wouldn't notice me.

I could still hear the dying gasps of 'Let It Be' echoing through the house. Poor Geoff must've been on his third encore by now. As he played the final notes, I realised the door hadn't creaked again. What was taking these two so long? How hard is it to fetch your coat and be on your way?

Listening intently, I began to panic as their murmuring grew louder: *were they getting closer, might I be seen?*

While I couldn't quite make out exact words or phrases, some sounds are unmistakable, even in the dark, even though the haze of a migraine. Like a zipper being unzipped, or a dress falling to the floor.

Goodness me, this must be a trick of the mind, I told myself – a terrifying side effect of the Naramig.

But then I heard someone exhale deeply. The louder their noises, the more I started to worry – not only was my head pounding, now my heart was too. A few more inches and I would be spotted. The idea of the conversation that might follow sent real chills up my spine. I simply couldn't risk being sprung, so I decided to quietly roll off the chaise longue, onto the floor and under the bed.

Kate had spared no expense, decorating the house with beautiful antique furniture, and the bed was no exception. Made with an ornate cast-iron frame – such superb craftsmanship – it sat high off the floor, allowing enough room for me to hide comfortably. She'd paid a tidy sum for it to be shipped from Normandy and I had admired it earlier from afar, unaware I would later admire it from beneath.

From my vantage point, all I could see were two sets of legs, the man's pants bunched around his ankles. Above me the mystery pair became emboldened, frantic. I screwed my eyes shut, but I failed to block my ears, a mistake that would haunt me forever and a day.

'Steph, YOU FEEL AMAZING!'

Steph. Steph, whose little hand I used to hold crossing the road. Steph who called from university every Sunday evening to ask after my weekend. Steph, my baby girl.

Oh, dear god, that's the voice of my only daughter, Steph.

What happened next seemed a gift from the heavens. First, I heard Kate's voice: 'And this up here is the master bedroom,' and then the light came on. 'You'll notice it has the same high ceilings as the rest of the –'

Silence.

From my floor-level view, I could make out Kate's legs by the door. I held my breath for what felt like an eternity before she backed out of the room, stuttering something about showing off her cellar.

Kate switched off the light and closed the door. It was just the three of us once more.

Thankfully it sounded as if Josh was getting dressed, clearly rattled by the close call. Every so often I could hear Steph's laugh – such a lovely laugh in the right context – followed by her soothing words to Josh. I wondered how I would ever look him in the eye again, or Steph for that matter.

For the sake of everyone involved, myself especially, I would simply have to put it out of my mind. Pack the whole ordeal up in a box and leave it there, under the dusty bed. Perhaps, with a little luck, the migraine might render the entire episode a hazy nightmare, a blurry memory roped to a sinking anchor.

Or perhaps not, I thought, as the bed groaned and sagged, hovering inches away from my face. Goodness me, they were staying; they were going again.

When Steph was young, five-going-on-six, the only book she wanted to read at night was *There's a Monster Under My Bed* by James Howe.

It was about a little boy called Simon, who'd convinced his mother he no longer needed a night-light now that he was all grown up. But on Simon's first night in the dark, his fear conjures something up.

'There's a monster under my bed, I can hear him breathing,' explains a fraught-looking Simon to his mum. 'Listen, I told you. There's a monster under my bed.'

Though it's been well over fifteen years since I last opened the book, I can still recite it word for word. One of those funny things about being a parent: whatever your child loves sticks in your brain, clings to the sides. I forget my co-workers' names almost weekly but ask me to recount which fruits the Very Hungry Caterpillar consumes from Monday to Friday, and I won't miss a beat.

'Mummy, do you think there are any monsters under my bed?' Steph would ask, wonderfully innocent.

'Of course not, sweetheart,' I would say, smoothing her hair and pretending to check beneath the bed. 'All clear!'

As she grew up, Steph continued to enjoy the book, but would often request we stop so she could offer her thoughts on the plot, and Simon in particular.

'Simon's silly,' she'd tell me, the years whizzing by in front of my eyes. 'He's a scaredy-cat! I wouldn't be afraid of any monsters under my bed.'

Oh Steph, but what if it wasn't a monster; what if it was your mother?

'Do you like that?' Josh's breathy voice forced me back into the reality I'd so desperately tried to ignore. 'I think you like that!'

Based on my daughter's groan, it sounded obvious that yes, she quite liked it, but apparently, Josh was unconvinced. 'Do you like it? You love it, don't you?' he probed once more.

Oh dear, how had I ended up here? One Naramig and a lie-down had turned into a *doyoulikeitdoyouloveit* romp starring my own flesh and blood.

And it was a romp that didn't appear to be wrapping up anytime soon. I was unsure how long had passed, but it felt like an age. Behold the vigour of youth!

Before Josh arrived on the scene, Steph had been seeing an older man by the name of Wilson. He was far too old for her, late forties I believe, but had dazzled her with his array of degrees and doctorates.

The first time I met Wilson, he remarked that we were 'almost of the same vintage', before offering out a spotty hand for me to shake. Needless to say, I didn't take to him after that.

Predictably, Wilson was a disaster, crushing Steph's confidence and breaking her heart. The dangers of dating outside your demographic. But all things considered, I missed Wilson greatly as I lay under the bed. For there's no way a man of his age would've possessed Josh's stamina.

On and on it went, the mattress drooping dangerously close to my face with every plunge.

Aside from the obvious psychological trauma, I had begun to fear for my physical safety. Kate hadn't exaggerated when describing the bed as a 'genuine antique', a nineteenth-century relic not designed for this type of strenuous thrusting.

With each movement it shuddered and shook, sounding perilously close to collapse – what a way to go; crushed under the weight of your fornicating daughter and her new boyfriend.

'Are we being too loud?' Steph whispered. Yes! Yes! Yes! You're being too *everything*, sweetheart. Put a stop to this madness, please.

'No, I don't think anyone will hear us over the music,' laughed Josh.

He was right, too: even from my sheltered position Cyndi Lauper's 'True Colours' was clearly audible, Kate singing along loudly, out of tune and out of time.

The most immediate problem I faced, quite literally, was the ancient and rusted bedsprings driving toward me like daggers. As the passion grew losing an eye became a real possibility.

Strangely, I found the safest thing to do was fall into step with their rhythm. Every time they went for it, I would kink my head to the side, narrowly avoiding being gored by a rusty spring.

It was around this moment that Josh resumed his intimate interrogation: 'Are you close? I'm close.'

Well, hurry up then! I thought.

It seemed my silent scolding worked; the bed began to shake more violently now. I tried my hardest to block out the noise: the words, the yelps of encouragement. Then came one last push, followed by an endless swapping of names.

'JOSH!'

'STEPH!'

'JOSH!'

'STEPH!'

Finally, it was done, and a quiet settled over the room, the three of us lying on our backs in the dark. Josh and Steph completely oblivious, me forever changed.

Eventually, I heard them dress and leave, the door creaking closed. For the first time in what seemed like hours, I let out a deep breath.

There's a mother under my bed. I can hear her breathing. Listen, I told you. There's a mother under my bed.

* * * * * * *

Epilogue

Two nights after Aunt Kate's housewarming, the entire Fitzgerald family gathered at a local pub, one last drink for the road.

Despite the half-hearted protests of 'we should do this more often!' and 'let's not leave it so long next time!' almost everyone knew that it would be a while before they were all in the same place again. Emotions ran high.

Even Uncle Ron was there; misty-eyed in the corner and nursing a schooner. Nothing like a family reunion to remind you of all that is important in life.

Among the hugs and back slaps, Steph and Josh exchanged smirks. Against all the odds, Aunt Kate had kept their secret from the rest of the family.

That's not to say she completely refrained from having her fun. On Saturday she'd slipped a note that read, 'Good morning rooters!' under their bedroom door. But aside from the occasional innuendo, Aunt Kate's lips stayed shut.

While much of the Fitzgerald family gave it a solid nudge that Sunday night, Steph and Josh took it easy. They had an early flight back to Geelong the next morning, and there's nothing worse than feeling dusty at the airport.

They sipped their beers slowly and unpacked the boring details of the week that lay ahead. Steph was going to Trivia with work friends on Tuesday night. Josh had something on Thursday.

Then Sandra approached and pulled up a seat, causing both Josh and Steph to stiffen slightly. They knew their secret was safe but still; Steph wondered if her mum had been quieter than usual, though that was normal after a migraine. Josh didn't know what to think.

'Josh,' said Sandra, looking the young man in the eyes

and opening her purse, 'go and get us three shots of tequila, will you?'

Sandra retrieved a fifty dollar note and handed it to him. The colour was draining from his face but doing as he was told, Josh left mother and daughter alone at the table.

Steph knew what was coming, but that didn't make the gut punch any easier to stomach.

'So, you know how I get migraines ...' began Sandra, looking down at the table. 'Well, on Friday night at Kate's I was feeling under the weather. I'd taken one of my tablets and I needed somewhere to lie down.'

In just enough detail to make Steph consider never having sex again, Sandra proceeded to deliver a blow-by-blow account of her experience. The interruption, the noises, the rusted springs.

Despite never intending to raise the 'romp' with her daughter, the secret had weighed heavily on Sandra all weekend.

And now, as she unburdened herself, she seemed to grow in her chair. Conversely, Steph appeared to shrink in hers, trying to simultaneously process the news while replaying everything she had said, done or asked for.

Watching Steph's face, Sandra suspected her daughter was in the middle of an internal meltdown, and she understood why. But she also knew that Steph was serious about

Josh, she could see it in her eyes, and if he was going to be hanging around, then it was best nothing remained unsaid.

It was at that moment Josh returned, balancing three shots of tequila on an aluminium tray.

Before he could speak, Sandra grabbed one and downed it, then turned to Steph.

'Now you tell him.'

THE F*** UP HALL OF FAME

An Expensive Case of Elbow Painting

Name: Steve Wynn   **Rating**: 10/10

Fuck-up: The day before selling an original Picasso for $139 million, casino mogul Steve Wynn had some buddies over to see the painting. Then he put his elbow through it.

It took Pablo Picasso just one afternoon to paint *La Rêve*, and it took Steve Wynn just one afternoon to ruin it.

On 24 January 1932, the legendary French artist was whiling the day away with his mistress, Marie-Thérèse Walter. He asked the striking 22-year-old to sit for a portrait, and in a fit of paint-splattered passion, desire spilled onto the canvas. Picasso would call the highly erotic piece *La Rêve* (*The Dream*).

But eventually one man's dream became another man's nightmare, with *La Rêve* leading to one of the most jaw-dropping fuck-ups of all time.

Picasso offloaded the piece in the 1940s and with each subsequent sale, the value skyrocketed. In 1997 it sold for

$48.4 million to Austrian-born investment fund manager Wolfgang Flöttl, making it the fourth-most expensive painting ever.

Four years later, Steve Wynn took it off Wolfgang's hands for a cool $60 million.

While the casino magnate was no stranger to expensive art, even he knew *La Rêve* was special. Something about the sexually charged portrait spoke to Wynn, so much so that in 2003 he decided to name his shiny new Las Vegas resort after the painting.

For reasons still unknown to outsiders, Wynn abandoned these plans soon after, deciding instead to name his resort Wynn Las Vegas – *how original*. By 2006 he was ready to part ways with the Picasso, and he already had an interested buyer in friend and fellow cashed-up collector Steven A. Cohen.

The billionaire buddies struck a deal: Cohen would pay US$139 million for it, the highest known price ever paid for a work of art. So much for mates' rates.

The night before the sale was finalised, Steve was catching up with friends at his Las Vegas resort. As we can all appreciate, when you're about to sell your favourite Picasso, you want to show it off before it's gone forever.

Steve whisked his pals up to a private office for a personal viewing. Sure, the artwork was on the brink of a world record sale, but what's the worst that could happen?

As the party gazed upon Picasso's handiwork, Steve began expounding on the painting, edging dangerously close to the frame. Now, when Steve was in his twenties, he was diagnosed with a rare eye defect, retinitis pigmentosa, which causes a loss of peripheral vision.

Basically, at certain angles, Steve can't see shit, and on this day, it just so happened that in his peripheral vision was *La Rêve*. Unaware of how close he was to the painting, Steve gestured expansively, puncturing the canvas with his right elbow.

Oh, to be a fly on the wall during that fuck-up. 'Well, I'm glad I did it and not you,' Steve reportedly said to his shell-shocked guests, while presumably having an internal meltdown.

The next day, Cohen walked from the deal and to make matters worse Steve's insurance company promptly revalued the artwork at $85 million. In one fell swoop, he had elbowed more than fifty million dollars off the original value.

Before you feel too sorry for Steve, like all plucky billionaires he managed to bounce back. After a meticulous restoration, Cohen decided he would buy the painting after all, shelling out for $155 million in 2013. Talk about a feel-good story.

Amazingly, Steve's Picasso curse wasn't over just yet. In 2018, he was set to auction off another of his collection, the artist's 1943 self-portrait, *Le Marin*. A day before it was due to go under the hammer (figuratively), a metal pole fell on the artwork (literally), tearing it.

Rumour has it the hole was so vast, Steve could've crawled inside and never come out.

Lost My Mind
(and Everything Else) in Madrid

Steven's story

To begin at the beginning makes the most sense, but if I've learned anything in my thirty-odd years on this earth, things don't always make sense.

Instead, my story starts at the beginning of the end with two men sitting opposite each another in an all-glass office.

We have Kenneth Broadhurst, terrifying alpha-boss, and one of the most successful current affairs TV producers in the game. And me, Steven Miller, nervous rookie and one of the most junior current affairs TV producers in the game.

You knew Kenneth was successful because he reminded

everyone all the time, but also because his office was a shrine to his accomplishments. Wherever you glanced, you found nods to a stellar career in journalism.

On the wall to my left hung framed newspaper clippings of important stories he'd broken next to pictures of Kenneth shaking hands with a variety of world leaders. To my right, faded snaps of a young Kenneth in a flak jacket on assignment in some war-torn country.

Then there was the collection of awards and trophies Kenneth proudly exhibited on shelves behind his desk: a gleaming reminder that he was a winner and you were not.

So regular were his wins that the shelves had started to buckle, sagging under the weight of Kenneth's constant achievements.

I often wondered at what point Kenneth might quit displaying his trophies and start multipurposing them – fashioning them into door stops, paperweights or even blunt weapons.

Kenneth himself looked a little like a trophy, complete with a perfectly spherical bald head and barrel chest. I could easily see him being handed out at award ceremonies, painted gold, holding a sword and shield and affixed to a solid base. *And the Kenneth goes to . . .*

On this particular day, there would be no awards, especially not for me.

'Steven, I need you to be honest with me,' said Kenneth, loosening his tie. It was only Wednesday morning, but the week had already taken a toll – on both of us.

'Don't try and pull the wool over my eyes; I wasn't born yesterday.'

This too was classic Kenneth. He was forever making it clear that his wisdom and experience outweighed yours; that he'd *been around the block* (a favourite saying of his), *seen it all and done it all* (another common catchphrase), and that *nothing surprised him any more*.

Hold your horses on that last one, Kenneth, you may be surprised yet.

'Can I get you anything before we begin?' he asked, opening a manila folder marked EXPENSES.

I told him no thanks. My stomach was in knots, and the jet lag was kicking in, so I felt too sick to eat or drink, though I was encouraged by this uncharacteristic show of kindness. Perhaps everything would be just fine?

'Not even a chorizo salad with warm potatoes on the side? *And a fucking 25 EURO glass of vermouth?*'

Kenneth pulled out a piece of paper from the expense folder and held it up in front of me. I could see the page was a mess of red pen and question marks: never a good sign. I shook my head. *Why did I have to order the vermouth?*

'Then let's get started,' seethed Kenneth.

'Tell me everything that happened, don't stop until you've reached the end and if I have any questions, I'll let you know.'

****

So we were filming that story about retirees packing up their lives and moving to Spain because it's dirt cheap. Remember? I pitched it a while ago, and you approved it last month.

Anyway, the shoot went really well. We spent about a week in Martos, which is three and a half hours from Madrid. Middle of nowhere. I personally wouldn't retire there, but the people we interviewed seemed to like it.

The crew was four in total: there was me as lead producer, plus Lisa, the reporter, and a Spanish cameraman and his sound guy.

To be honest, by the time we wrapped on the final day, we were exhausted. Not only is Martos hard to get to but whoever sorted our accommodation booked somewhere an hour and a half away. Actually, I wanted to ask you: who is in charge of booking travel for producers?

You're right, it's not important at this moment, but maybe we can circle back? Or not. Let's forget it.

Because all the talent were elderly, they wanted to start shooting first thing in the morning, like six o'clock. A 6 am start meant getting up at 4 am and travelling to Martos, working all day and then driving back to our accommodation in the afternoon.

All I'm saying is we clocked up some travel time and it took a toll, but we got the job done. Once the story was in the can, well, you know what it's like when you've wrapped a shoot like that. You need to debrief and decompress, usually over a bottle of wine.

That night the four of us shared a few decent local drops, and then I called last drinks around midnight because we had to fly out the next day.

It was going to be an early start, too. While I was on a 10 pm flight, Lisa had booked a midday one. As I said, it was a three-hour drive from Martos to Madrid, but we wanted to allow four hours because we didn't want to be in a rush. Pretty responsible decision-making, no?

By 5 am we're on the road to make sure we arrive at the airport by 9 am so Lisa could make her flight. I know people talk a lot about the Autobahn in Germany being bad, but the Spanish highways are a special kind of hell. It's like 'choose your own adventure' over there. Everyone does 180 kilometres an hour, and there are no lines and no rules. It's just survive or don't.

I was stressed out of my mind trying to concentrate, but I was so tired that I had to do that thing where you put all the windows down and pump the music up just to stay awake. Full-blown sensory overload, wind in my face, Spanish hip-hop blasting through the car.

Are you a fan of Spanish hip-hop? Not really? Well, after four hours, consider me a convert.

Miraculously, we arrived at the airport safely and after returning the hire car I said goodbye to Lisa and off she went to London. It was 10 am. My flight was at 10 pm; I had twelve hours to kill.

Madrid is up there with my favourite cities in the world. I've been a bunch of times and I'll always go back. They say when it comes to Spain, you either prefer Madrid or Barcelona: you have a preference? I see you as a Madrid man. Am I right?

With time on my hands, I got the bus into town and headed straight for Mercado de San Miguel. You can't be disappointed by the San Miguel Mercado, hands-down best tapas in Madrid.

I fuelled up there and went for a walk, but by late afternoon I was peckish again, so I called ahead to see if I could score a table at Botin, one of the world's oldest restaurants.

A lot of places claim to be the world's oldest restaurant, though I'm pretty sure Botin really is. Either way, it sells the world's best suckling pig – and that's not up for debate.

Of course, I got a table no worries because it was only 4 pm, which meant the true Spaniards were mid-siesta.

I probably should've taken a leaf out of their book, but instead, I pushed myself to the next meal.

As has been my style forever, I over-ordered once I got to Botin. Warm bread to start, anchovies for entree and then the suckling pig for main. The waiter tried desperately to explain that the dish is designed to be shared between two. I ate it all.

Add to this heavy meal, two glasses of my favourite vermouth and what you have are the perfect conditions for a nap: very full, very sleepy.

When I suckled the last bit of pig off the plate, it was edging on 6 pm, so I cabbed it back to the airport. Check-in was smooth, and I made the gate with plenty of time to spare. There weren't any seats, so I grabbed a spot at a nearby airport restaurant.

I wasn't that hungry, but you know when you're so bored that you eat to entertain yourself? That was how I felt when I ordered the chorizo salad with warm potatoes, the one you mentioned earlier . . . plus another glass of red.

Yes, I agree it was all unnecessary.

I finished the meal – sorry, the *unnecessary meal* – and walked back to my gate. Still no seats, meaning I had to sit around the corner. I checked my phone; it read 8.30 pm.

My day had started at 4 am and included driving to the airport, tapas at the Mercado, suckling pig for two, a chorizo salad, and too much vermouth. Tired was an understatement.

Rather than risk watching a movie on my computer and falling asleep, I decided to listen to my Ancient Rome podcast. Are you a podcast guy? I've really got into them lately. I can send some recommendations through if you're interested.

Sorry, yes, I know we're not here to talk podcasts.

Anyway, I put my Bose QC35 noise-cancelling headphones on, pushed play and settled in.

Never did I think to set the alarm because I was physically on my phone, sending emails, texting the family. What I'm saying is: *my eyes were wide open . . . until they weren't.*

Next thing I knew I woke up facedown on the floor like I'd been executed by the mob.

Zero idea how I ended up there. Thankfully my phone was in my pocket, some muscle memory must've slid it in as I drifted off. Checked the time: midnight.

The plane I was supposed to be on had left two hours ago. All I could think was: *I'm fucked. That's it. I'm fucked.* But that realisation was almost immediately replaced by an even worse one: all my stuff was gone.

My backpack had been resting on my lap and inside was my laptop, all the audio and vision we'd filmed, plus my passport. All gone.

Honestly, I don't mean to sound dramatic, I know you've been in war zones and stuff, but it was just *so* heartbreaking.

I've never felt so alone. The airport was empty, I'd missed my flight, and someone had stolen my bag.

All I could do was walk around in a daze, moaning 'Hello? Hello? *Olaaaaa? Ollaaaaa?*'

Finally I stumbled across this cute elderly cleaning lady pushing a trolley, so I Googled the Spanish word for 'backpack' – which is *mochila* by the way – and I'm yelling *mochila* at this poor woman.

She didn't understand but seemed delightful, so I followed her and she led me to a sign that read, *Seguridad de Aeropuerto*: Airport Security.

Maybe Airport Security would be my saviour. Maybe they had my bag? Maybe they'd taken it during my impromptu nap? Maybe the worst-case scenario was that I'd missed the flight and I could catch the next one?

Maybe I would never have to sit in front of my boss and explain what happened. Maybe?

I couldn't have been more wrong. Things were about to take a turn for the worse.

* * * * * * *

'Stop there,' Kenneth said, massaging his temples.

He had further loosened his tie and undone the first button of his shirt; at this rate he would be nude by the time I finished my story.

'Okay, I have a question for you.'

Kenneth looked exhausted by everything he'd heard so far, which didn't bode well because we had a way to go.

'Just let me clarify a few things first,' he added, leafing through the documents on his desk. 'After treating yourself to a solo food and wine tour of Madrid's famous ... was it the San Fernando market?'

'San Miguel,' I corrected.

'Right, San Miguel. Once you're finished at San Miguel, you then visit some old restaurant?'

Don't say it, Steven, just leave it. 'World's oldest restaurant.'

If looks could kill, Kenneth was a murderer. 'At this place you eat another meal which is charged to your corporate card: 150 euros plus tip?'

That all sounds pretty accurate. 'Yes.'

'Now correct me if I'm wrong, though I rarely am,' continued Kenneth. 'Finally, you decide to return to the airport, where you inexplicably order a third meal and another glass of wine.'

Can't fault the timeline. 'That's right.'

'A short time later you fall asleep, missing the flight home that we paid for, and everything you own is stolen.'

'Not everything,' I countered. As a news buff, it's important Kenneth sticks to the facts. 'I still had my phone and wallet on me. And my noise-cancelling headphones!'

'Right, but your backpack is gone and inside that backpack were the original tapes of the story you'd just spent a week shooting in regional Spain? Is that correct?'

I nodded.

'My question for you is this: *where were the backups?*'

Desperation rattled in his voice. I suspected another button would soon be undone.

'No producer worth his salt would dream of keeping all the copies in one place,' fumed Kenneth.

'Funny you should mention the backups, Kenneth, allow me to explain.'

* * * * * * *

After the cleaner dropped me off at Airport Security, I came up with a two-pronged plan.

First: review the security cameras to see what happened when I fell asleep.

Second: track down my checked baggage because – *drumroll* – that's where the backup tapes were!

Like you said, any producer worth his salt . . .

So, I'm trying to relay this two-pronged plan to two security guards, but they weren't having it.

The gist was that they can't access CCTV without police permission and that retrieving my checked baggage was impossible because it was one o'clock in the morning and the airport was effectively closed.

I'm thinking, okay, this is a bit of a nightmare, but I'll check into an airport hotel, grab some sleep and –

– Yeah, you're right, I should've been well-rested. No, I don't think it's a medical thing; I was just exhausted.

Like I was saying, I assumed I'd be sent to a hotel, but then the guards surrounded me, and suddenly, I was being led to this weird area at the back of the airport. You know: like on those airport security shows when they take those poor suckers into the underbelly of the building and you can tell they're in deep shit? It was like that.

Didn't you work on one of those programs for a bit? Yeah, so you know exactly what I mean.

We get to this terrifying room, and one of the guys lays it out: 'You cannot leave the airport because you do not have your passport and we forbid you to enter Spain. It is forbidden!'

You can imagine my confusion. I was so distressed that all I could offer was a high pitched *WHAT?*

He repeats: 'You cannot leave!'

WHAT?

He keeps going: 'You must stay with us until further notice.'

WHAT?

And finally: 'Leave your belongings here and follow me.'
WHAT?

He points to an empty tub where I have to 'deposit my phone and wallet', literally my last two worldly possessions. Then he hands me a half-sized bottle of water plus a set of sheets and leads me to a small room, let's call it a cell, with lino floors and bunk beds.

I'm talking about proper prison vibes, like I wanted to start carving into the wall: DAY ONE.

Yes, I understand it's not the same as an actual prison. No, I've never seen the story you shot at Abu Ghraib.

The point I'm making is that it was a bit much. I reckon I spent a solid hour screaming, 'I HAVE NOT COMMITTED A CRIME!', but no one was listening. Eventually, I made my sad bunk bed, took a sip of rationed water and – you'll hate this next bit – fell asleep again.

Yes, I know you don't get it, but sleep is actually a type of survival mode. If you're in shock or whatever, the body shuts down. Yep, sorry, I'll continue.

A few hours later, I wake to rapid Spanish being spoken and open my cell door to see a bunch of guys sitting at a long communal table playing cards. I'd later learn they were illegal immigrants from Peru who had entered Spain using fake documents.

So they all stop and look up at me, and I'm looking back at them and we're in the middle of this staring contest when the security doors open and in struts this super-tanned guy with crazy white teeth, slicked-back hair and he's wearing a three-piece suit.

He introduces himself as the Airport Police Liaison Officer, but he looked more like a Latin American Bond Villain to me.

Soon as he enters, I go to speak but he puts his finger up to his lips: 'I will deal with you, *un momento.*' He then starts screaming at the Peruvians, who scatter in fear.

After about five minutes, I'm summoned from my room, and he asks me to explain what happened. I tell him the whole sob story from beginning to end.

Yes, I mentioned the world's oldest restaurant. No, I left out the chorizo salad.

I'm back at square one: trying to relay my two-pronged plan, explaining that I need to review the tapes and I *must* track down my checked baggage. 'Impossible' was his immediate response.

Then he totally panics me by asking: 'Where is your lawyer?' Again, I return to my faithful answer: *WHAT?* He's shaking his head at me and saying, '*Señor*, we cannot proceed with the investigation until I meet with your lawyer.'

WHAT INVESTIGATION? WHAT LAWYER? I haven't hurt anyone or smuggled anything! I fell asleep; my biggest crime is that I like to nap!

At this point, we're both getting angry and he just keeps repeating the word 'protocol': 'A lawyer is protocol, an investigation is protocol, the consulate is protocol.'

In the middle of his protocol speech, there's a knock on the door and the cute little cleaner walks in with her trolley.

Yes, exactly! The one who found me after I fell asleep.

Next thing you know she is hurling abuse at him, though all I can make out is *mochila*, which means 'backpack', like I told you earlier. Her tongue-lashing goes on for a while before he turns back to me, all sheepish and says, wait for it: 'My *mamá* tells me she helped you last night.'

HIS MOTHER. THE CLEANER IS HIS MOTHER.

Sorry, I didn't mean to yell, it's just . . . unreal scenes.

Now that *Mamá*'s in charge, things start to move quickly. Within ten minutes, the embassy in Madrid have faxed over a copy of my original passport while confirming they will provide me with an emergency passport that I can use to fly home.

Talk about getting shit done! *Mamá* is on fire.

Yes, perhaps you should've hired her instead. No, I don't know if she's had much experience producing television.

Sensing *Mamá* is my best shot at finding my luggage. I get her son to translate and tell *Mamá* that I need to visit the Emirates desk and check if anyone has my bag. She just smiles and said '*Sígueme*', which I think means 'follow me' or 'this way'.

We end up at the baggage claim, which is a total ghost town in the early morning, but in the distance I spy a single blob on the carousel. Surely not?

I run over, and there it stands in all its glory: my red suitcase. Flight crew must've dumped it off the plane when I didn't board, and it just sat there doing laps all night.

Unzip the bag and what's the first thing I see? The backups. Safe as houses, never in doubt.

****

'Stop there,' sighed Kenneth. 'Please, just stop.'

Quick outfit update: Kenneth has removed the tie completely, and three buttons are undone. He no longer looks crushed by my incompetence but instead more closely resembles a used car salesman at the end of a long, and unproductive, day.

'You're telling me you've had the backup tapes this whole time?'

Yes, I nodded, grabbing the tapes from my bag and laying them out across his desk. Kenneth's face blushed into a deep purple.

'Why on earth wouldn't you open with that?' he asked, snatching the tapes and stuffing them in a drawer. 'Journalism 101: *Don't bury the lead!*'

'But, but –' I could feel myself slipping. The jet lag, chorizo and vermouth were combining to bring me down at my most vulnerable moment.

'BUT WHAT?' roared Kenneth.

'– but you also said, "Tell me everything that happened and don't stop until you've reached the end" and that part only comes right at the end.'

Reminder to self: don't remind Kenneth of things he said.

'I know what I said,' he replied softly, which was arguably more intimidating. 'Honestly, how do you even . . . where do I even . . . *I can't even* . . .'

As his sentences dissolved into broken whispers, I silently prayed for the meeting to be over. I couldn't handle another unbuttoned outburst – time to angle for the wrap-up.

'The important thing is that the tapes are safe,' I said, collecting my bag and standing up from my chair. 'And that our story can still go to air.'

'Sit,' demanded Kenneth. He opened the dreaded EXPENSES folder once more and retrieved another piece of paper massacred by red pen.

'The Westin Palace Madrid,' he began. 'Three nights in a *three-bedroom villa.*'

Kenneth's eyes bulged as he continued reading. 'Plus, room service on night one *and* room service on night two, bringing the total expenditure to,' he paused a moment, '1600 euros!'

'I know that seems excessive,' I replied. 'But I actually *saved* the company money.'

'Are you familiar with *Fiesta Nacional de España*?'

Kenneth shook his head.

'No, neither was I. Let me clear up the confusion.'

* * * * * * *

Having secured the tapes, my attention turned to getting home. My original flight left on the Friday but, of course, I'd slept through that, woken up on the ground and spent the rest of the night in my cell.

Fine, it wasn't a cell. A room, with a bunk bed … that locked from the outside.

Anyway, now it's Saturday and in Spain no one does anything on the weekends.

The embassy was open but skeleton staff only, so when I turn up to organise my emergency passport, there's just one confused guy behind the desk. He looks about twelve years old, too; surely that's illegal?

He and I go back and forth for a bit, but it's clear I'm going nowhere fast.

Yes, I agree: that is a real running theme for me on this trip.

The embassy guy then explains that my only hope is to return on Tuesday to get my emergency passport. Tuesday, I ask, confused. Why can't I come back on Monday?

Oh, because Monday is *Fiesta Nacional de España*, he says. Spain's national holiday.

You thought the weekend was bad? The whole country takes the day off for this thing. Good luck getting anywhere.

Not only am I now stuck in Madrid for another three days, but what happens when I go to book myself into a hotel? Or a motel? Or anything? SOLD OUT, FULL, NO *VACÁNTE*.

People have travelled from all over Spain to celebrate and the city is rammed.

My embassy buddy could probably tell I was about to explode because he makes a few calls and tells me he's managed to find a room at The Westin Palace. Apparently, that's where diplomats stay when they're in Madrid.

Yes, I know I'm not a diplomat.

But if you look up prices for a three-bedroom villa at The Westin Palace, it's usually double what they charged me. Sorry, charged you. Sorry, charged *the company*. If anything, we made a saving on this part of the trip? Could've been much worse, almost a silver lining?

You're right. I know you're not in the mood to look for silver linings.

And that's pretty much it. I spent the next three days getting a head start on the story. I also managed to file a police report which means the company can claim everything back on travel insurance – another saving.

And yes, I did order some room service but only because I thought it was safer than venturing out. After everything I'd been through, I was convinced that if I left my room . . .

Sorry, yes, *villa*.

If I left my *villa*, then something terrible would happen. I'd be mugged or drugged or gored by a running bull.

Tuesday arrived, the embassy rushed through the passport, and I caught the next flight out.

Touched down yesterday and here I am today, sitting in front of you, Kenneth.

* * * * * * *

This time Kenneth didn't tell me to stop because the story was done, I'd reached the end of the end. He stood up in front of me, imposing.

'Steven, as you know, I've been around the block, seen it all, done it all,' explained Kenneth, gesturing to the many awards behind him.

'And after everything I've experienced in my life, nothing surprises me any more.' He took a minute to roll his sleeves up. 'But this takes the cake.'

I prepared for the onslaught, instead Kenneth's face softened, and he thrust his hand out in front of me. 'Go home, take the day and let's never, *ever*, speak of this again.'

'Thank you, Kenneth,' I said, shaking his outstretched hand. 'I could really use a nap.'

THE F*** UP HALL OF FAME

Almost a Beatle

Name: Pete Best   **Rating**: 6/10

Fuck-up: Getting fired from the Beatles in 1962, a year before they became the biggest rock and roll band of all time.

There's a delicious irony to the fact that the Beatles' back catalogue is full of songs that are ideally suited to anyone who just lost their job.

Got the boot from your local pizzeria? *Let It Be*.

Office manager said your services are no longer required? *I Feel Fine*.

Bank account looking dangerously empty? *All You Need Is Love*.

Stayed up all night drowning your sorrows after getting the hook? *Here Comes the Sun*.

But for Pete Best, the drummer who was fired by the Beatles months before they became the most influential band of all time, no tune will ever truly capture the crushing disappointment.

Except maybe . . . *Help!*

In early 1960, John Lennon, Paul McCartney and George Harrison were kicking around Liverpool making a splash with their raucous brand of rock and roll. At the time they were known as Beatals and would experiment with several variations of the name (and spelling) until finally settling on the Beatles.

In August that year, the three-piece hired Pete Best, who had previously been drumming for another local band, the Blackjacks. Best proved to be the missing piece of the puzzle, and with a drummer on deck the Beatles hightailed it to Germany for their first-ever residency. On 17 August, the Beatles played their debut gig with Best at the Indra Club in Hamburg.

The Hamburg shows would become legendary in Beatles folklore as the band gathered momentum. Over the next two years, the hype around the band continued to swell and by 1962 there was little doubt they were the Next Big Thing™.

In June they signed a deal with EMI, one of the most influential record labels in the UK, and began laying down tracks at EMI's Abbey Road studios in London.

During initial recording sessions, legendary producer George Martin reportedly didn't think Best was up to scratch and suggested hiring a session drummer for the remainder of the album.

This played perfectly into the hands of John, Paul and George, who had recently started to turn on poor old Pete and were looking for an excuse to punt him from the band.

The reasons for their about-face remain up for debate, though Best has long promoted the story that John, Paul and Ringo were jealous of his good looks. (Admittedly this is exactly the type of rumour you would spread once you'd been booted.)

There were apparently also whispers that Best was a loner and his refusal to embrace the Beatles' way of life, including ridiculous LEGO-looking haircut, bristled his bandmates.

Anyway, after George Martin criticised Best's drumming, Paul, John and George promptly tasked their manager, Brian Epstein, with turfing him from the band.

On Thursday 16 August 1962, almost two years to the day since his first show as a Beatle, Pete Best was fired. By the weekend they'd already lined up his replacement in Ringo Starr.

One year after his dismissal the Beatles hit number one in the UK with their song, 'She Loves You', marking the beginning of Beatlemania. By that time, Pete Best was working as a civil servant in Liverpool.

While Best's firing is certainly a fuck-up of the highest order, it's not all bad news for the unluckiest man in music. In 1995, the Beatles released *Anthology 1*, which included ten tracks featuring Best on drums. He received a payout reported to be more than £1 million from the sale.

And just like everything in life, there's a Beatles song for that too: *Money (That's What I Want)*.

The Flight From Hell

Megan's story

'This is the final boarding call for passengers Megan and Jack Heywood booked on flight 372A to Tucson, Arizona. Please proceed to gate three immediately. Last checks are being completed, and the captain will order for the doors of the aircraft to close in approximately five minutes. I repeat. This is the final boarding call for Megan and Jack Heywood. Thank you.'

I looked down at tiny Jack Heywood, strapped to my chest and screaming for his life. Did they really want him on the plane that much?

'This is the final call.' The booming voice belonged to a compact blonde flight attendant with a clipped southern accent, Texan probably. From my seat, I could see her perched awkwardly on a stool, unconsciously smoothing out her skirt. Like everyone who worked at the airport, she wore a plastered-on smile that didn't falter.

'REPEAT, final call, the gate is closing. We are paging Megan and Jack Heywood *again*.'

We were the only two left at the gate, the stampede of passengers had passed us, but I remained anchored to my seat. Finally, the attendant gave up and walked over to me.

'Are you Megan Heywood?' I nodded. 'Excuse me ma'am, but we've been paging you for the last fifteen minutes. You're holding everyone up, do you understand?'

I wanted to tell her that I did understand, explain that I wasn't an inconsiderate person. I was just tired, so very, very tired. But then Jack started wailing again and the moment passed.

'Boarding pass?' She held out a freshly manicured hand. A name tag pinned to her uniform read 'Kristy'. Kristy had perfect hair; I hadn't washed mine in weeks.

'Ah yes, boarding pass, it's just … somewhere,' I said, patting down my pockets in vain.

'Would you like me to help you find it?' smiled Kristy. I nodded again. With ruthless efficiency, she searched my bags, quickly retrieving two crinkled boarding passes.

'Always in the last place you look,' she said, straining to be heard over Jack's latest breakdown.

'You and your son are in row C, travel time is around ninety minutes, have a lovely flight, and god bless!'

I'm not a religious person, but as Jack and I made our way down the jet bridge and onto the plane, I offered up a prayer to whoever might be listening. *Please let this next bit go okay.*

* * * * * * *

Eighteen hours earlier

'And you've got the extra nappies?' asked Chris, frantically ticking items off his list. My husband loves to make lists and then check them off.

'Yes, I have the extra nappies,' I said, rocking Jack in my arms. He was four months old, I'd had four minutes of sleep in the last four days, but yes, I was certain I had packed the extra nappies.

'Well, why aren't they crossed off the list?'

Travelling presented Chris with the ideal platform to scratch his list itch, and when we decided to fly halfway around the world with a four-month-old baby, he went into a list frenzy.

I say *we* decided. I mean my mom decided. Chris had barely finished cutting Jack's umbilical cord when she started harassing us to visit the family in Arizona.

THE FLIGHT FROM HELL

'I don't even know what it feels like to hold my grandson!' she cried down the phone as I booked our tickets from Sydney to Arizona. 'Am I even a real grandmother if I haven't met him yet?'

Most parents might warm up to the long-haul trip, maybe start small by going interstate, but not us. Our first ever flight with Jack, and we were doing fourteen hours from Sydney to Los Angeles, then another two from LA to Arizona. Go big or go home, or in this case, go big *and* go home.

Because we were so paranoid about forgetting something, we decided to bring everything. Chris resembled a packhorse as we boarded the plane in Sydney, swaying down the aisle crashing into people. 'Sorry, I'm so sorry, sorry, oh whoops, my bad.'

It may have been our maiden voyage as travelling parents, but I already understood it required a lot of apologising to strangers. 'Sorry,' we chorused when Chris nearly decapitated the woman sitting in front of us.

Despite the fuss Jack's eyes remained shut, I tapped Chris, but he ignored me in favour of triple-checking his carry-on. For all his military-like preparation, Chris is prone to panic, and he'd dropped the ball big time during Jack's birth.

He had taken it upon himself to meticulously pack my hospital bag, but in the whirlwind of 'holy shit here comes the baby!' he'd grabbed his gym bag instead. Who needs handpicked essential oils when you've got a sweat towel and a pair of old Nikes?

He'd been scarred ever since.

'Everything locked and loaded!' said Chris, as he triumphantly unzipped his carry-on to reveal half the contents of our house. I was impressed that he managed to fit so much into such a small space.

Inside the bag were our spare sets of clothes, two different medicine cases and a special folder for our passports. Then there were several bottles of my finest breast milk chilling in a freezer bag. Plus baby Panadol, regular Panadol, ibuprofen, snacks, an iPad, books and headphones.

No doubt we'd gone overboard – did Jack need six different books? – but as a rookie mom, the illusion of being in control is just as important as actually being in control. We were prepared, we had our lists, nothing had been left to chance.

As the plane took off, and Sydney slipped away behind us, Jack barely even stirred. Satisfied with how things had panned out, Chris kissed Jack's forehead and reclined his seat.

'See, nothing to worry about, he's a dream.'

****

'According to the map it's only a mile and a half to In-N-Out from Terminal 7,' said Chris, staring intently at his phone. 'Though it looks like the walk takes you along a fairly busy highway.'

The second we touched down in Los Angeles, I started craving a burger. For all the amazing things Australia has to offer – universal healthcare, pleasant weather, Chris and Liam Hemsworth – no one does heart-stopping fast food better than Americans.

While I was happy to settle for an overpriced yet undercooked airport burger, Chris knew that I regularly fantasised about In-N-Out and he was in the mood to win me over. You see, the thing I haven't told you is that while we had planned this trip together, I had to finish it alone. Our visit to the States coincided with the start of the US Masters in Georgia, a bucket list event for golf-mad Chris.

I'd already known this when I booked the flights and wondered how long it would take for him to arrive at the same conclusion.

'You know what's crazy?' he said one day, flopping onto our bed and staring at the ceiling.

Whenever Chris suspected a topic was going to be met with resistance, he would try to bring it up as coolly as possible, as if it was just occurring to him at that moment.

Then he'd ruin it by going into too much detail, making it clear he'd done his research.

'You know what's crazy ... the Masters are on at the same time we're going to see your family! We could fly to Los Angeles together; I could pop over to Georgia, catch the first two days of play, and be back in Tucson by the weekend!'

At first, I feigned shock that he would rather watch golf than spend an extra forty-eight hours with my big American family, but ultimately I said yes, watch your stupid golf.

Which explains why he was now considering crossing six lanes of traffic to get me a burger.

'I reckon I can do it in half an hour.' Chris consulted his watch. 'My flight leaves at 2, your flight leaves a little after 3, we have more than enough time.'

'Honey, it's fine,' I said. 'I don't need In-N-Out, and you don't need to stress about leaving us, everything is under control.'

And it was true; the first leg went by without issue. Jack and Chris slept most of the way while I watched eighteen episodes of early-era Kardashians. We'd conquered the hard part; the rest should be a cakewalk.

'Well at least let me get you all set up?' offered Chris, returning to his first love, packing and unpacking. He busied himself with our bags, making sure I had all the essential

THE FLIGHT FROM HELL

baby paraphernalia required to keep Jack alive and, more importantly, happy.

'Wala is going in your backpack.' Chris held up Jack's favourite toy, a stuffed koala my mom had sent over. Like most Americans, she grossly overestimated how much of a role koalas played in our day-to-day life.

'So are your passports,' Chris said, zipping up the bag. 'Oh, and there's a spare dummy in the nappy bag, which is packed away in the pram!'

And with that, three became two, Chris bidding us a tearful farewell. 'I'm going to miss you guys so much, but I'll see you on Saturday!'

If I'd known what was coming, I would've cried too.

****

Gate 3, Terminal 3, Los Angeles Airport
Having navigated the maze that is LAX, we arrived at our gate with a couple of minutes to spare. Timed to perfection, right? Wrong.

'ATTENTION: All passengers travelling on flight 372A to Tucson, Arizona,' buzzed the overhead announcement. 'Your flight has been delayed due to a mechanical issue.'

Urgh. Despite being too young to understand that airlines, like golf-loving husbands, will always disappoint you,

Jack's reaction to the delay was entirely fitting: an angry and sustained cry.

'It's okay, beautiful boy,' I said to him, his heavy lids matching my own, 'it won't be long.' The lie escaped my lips with ease. That's the other thing I'd learnt about parenting – along with apologising, it also involved a lot of lying; lying to yourself, to your child, to the world.

The update sent people scurrying back to their seats. I scanned the area, looking for a spot to settle among the power suits and frazzled families, but no luck. Just as I was about to give up searching, the blunt shock of an Australian accent demanded my attention.

'Over here,' beckoned a smiling woman with a friendly face. 'G'day, I'm Janine.'

I immediately recognised her as Janine Shepherd, a former champion cross-country skier. While training for the 1988 Winter Olympics, she was hit by a truck and nearly killed. Only two weeks earlier Chris and I had watched her TED talk about overcoming adversity. Doctors told Janine she'd never walk again, yet here she was, striding towards me.

'Come, come, sit,' Janine said, clearing a space for Jack and me. 'Bloody Americans, they're hopeless! Experts at ignoring whatever is going on around them.'

'You're not wrong,' I agreed, trying not to recall how many bones Janine shattered in the accident.

We found common ground swapping notes on the differences between our two adopted countries. Janine was like me in reverse, born in Australia, but living in America.

'Wyoming is home now,' she said, rubbing her shoulders as if the mere mention of her freezing hometown triggered a cold shiver. 'But I travel a lot on the motivational speaking circuit.'

I had wondered if I was allowed to ask about the accident and this felt like a window, but then Janine promptly slammed it shut. 'Sydney to Arizona,' she said, stretching out her legs and peering inside the pram. 'That's a big trip for a little boy.'

'Blame his grandmother,' I explained. 'She couldn't go another day without meeting her grandson.'

'Well I don't blame her at all, look at this handsome man. You're a handsome boy, aren't you?' she cooed. 'How old is he?'

'Four months,' I replied, suddenly realising just how fresh he was, how long we had to go.

'It's such a beautiful age, don't you think?' Janine asked, flashing a practised smile.

This is the part where I'm supposed to agree, isn't it? 'Yes, beautiful. Exhausting, but beautiful.'

Before long we settled into a comfortable quiet. Jack drifted off while I hovered somewhere between conscious and comatose. Every so often I'd slip into a dead sleep, then violently jerk myself back into the land of the living.

'Hey, you need the rest too,' Janine told me. 'If he wakes up, I'll let you know.'

With Janine's permission, I let the tired take over. At one point, I registered Jack's muffled cry and forced opened my eyes – in a barely awake blur I could make out Janine bending down, picking him up and rocking him back to sleep. My guardian angel at Gate 3.

After an hour, I woke to an airline update. 'Attention, all passengers on flight 372A to Tucson, Arizona.'

A ripple of excitement fluttered through the gate – could it be our time? Opposite me, a man in a suit gripped his boarding pass like a winning lottery ticket.

'We understand your frustration and are doing everything in our power to fix the problem.'

Deflated, he slumped back in his chair, and inane chatter filled the air once more.

'Feeling better?' Janine's genuine concern sent a warm flush to my face, and I fought the urge to hug her and not let go.

'Much better, thanks.'

A look of mutual appreciation flashed between us, and for a moment, I pictured a future where Janine and I were best friends. 'It's the craziest story,' I'd tell people when they asked how I met the former ski champ. 'We were both delayed at LAX!'

My daydream came crashing down when Jack shit his nappy. 'Looks like our little man has conquered his first bout of travel-constipation,' said Janine, passing Jack my way.

The eye-watering smell was proof enough though I peeked inside just to be sure. There it was, a well-contained crime scene. Our exchange was interrupted by the buzz of *yet another* announcement.

'ATTENTION: All passengers flying to Jackson Hole, Wyoming,' crackled the PA system. 'We are now ready for boarding.'

'That's me.' Janine placed a hand on my shoulder and squeezed. Emotions are never far away when you're in the throes of new motherhood, and Janine's timely kindness combined with her sudden departure cracked me down the middle.

Tears pooled in the corners of my eyes as she gathered her things.

'Don't you cry,' warned Janine, switching into motivational speaking mode. 'I know you're tired, I know you feel alone, but you're going to get through this! This little man is lucky to have you as his mother. I'm telling you; you've got this!'

I could see why she was such a hit on the circuit, but Janine's pep talk only made me sob harder. Here was a woman who had literally had her dreams – and bones, and spine – crushed, yet she was counselling me about a cranky baby with a full nappy.

'You've got this, I know it. Megan the super mum, okay? Safe travels!'

As she walked away, Jack's cry hit a crescendo which was ideal actually, because it took the heat off me.

****

Under the unforgiving halogen lights of the airport bathroom, the full scope of Jack's shit-uation revealed itself. 'Jack, wow,' I said, unwrapping the nappy and holding my breath. By now I was largely desensitised to poop, but occasionally he'd serve up something that warranted a reaction. 'Fuck me.'

Instinctively, I checked over my shoulder. Chris and I had agreed not to swear in front of Jack, though he was halfway to Georgia so I figured all bets were off. 'That's a real doozy.' Jack grinned back at me: yes, that's right, Mother, some of my best work.

I had the nappy routine down to a fine art, and we worked together in perfect harmony. Jack offered his tiny ankles up, I scooped them together in one hand, wielding a wet wipe in the other.

'There we go, all better and let's never talk of this again,' I said, tossing the napalm nappy into the bin.

I gave Jack a final once over and then reached down for the nappy bag which Chris had so diligently packed away in the undercarriage of the pram. *Except he hadn't.*

Sitting in the spot where the nappy bag was supposed to be was a small zip-up case, a golf ball emblem stitched on the outside. *Not again, Chris, please not again.*

I already knew what was inside, but I opened the bag anyway: two golf gloves, a thousand loose tees, Chris's hideous Nike DRI-Fit golf polo shirt, but not a single nappy. *This can't be happening.*

Besides Jack's actual NAPPIES, the nappy bag was home to several crucial baby bits and pieces: dummy, wet wipes, portable change mat, rash cream. All these items had been ticked off Chris's godforsaken list but what's the point of even *having* a list when you take the wrong bag?

In a manic frenzy I tore the pram apart, but it was over. Somewhere in the sky, flying over the great state of Georgia, a clueless Chris was heading to the Masters with a whole bunch of nappies.

The no-swearing rule was promptly cancelled. 'Jack, I'm sorry to tell you,' I fumed, shifting his nude body from one hip to the other. 'But your father is a fucking idiot.'

Having already cried once in public that day, I was determined not to break again. 'You've got this, Megan,' I told myself, repeating Janine's words.

Using Chris's polo, I fashioned a makeshift nappy, not feeling a single shred of guilt at the possibility it might soon be soiled.

'Daddy won't mind if you dirty his golf shirt,' I explained to Jack.

'Because Daddy won't be going golfing ever again.'

Now to solve this problem.

First thought: can you buy nappies in an airport?

Back in the terminal, I moved at pace, hitting all the surrounding stores in a hysteric panic: 'Do you sell nappies?' Most shopkeepers replied with a dismissive shake of the head. Only one brave soul dared talk back. 'Don't you mean diapers, lady?' Urgh.

With each mounting no, I cursed the goddamn patriarchy. Only in a world made by men, for men can you buy a five-thousand-dollar watch and a six-litre bottle of whiskey – *from the same store* – but no freaking nappies.

Just as I prepared to do the unthinkable – try my luck in another terminal – this happened: 'Attention all passengers.' *Don't you say it, don't you dare.* 'Flight 372A to Tucson, Arizona, is now ready for boarding.'

To my left was the gate, to my right was the parents'

room, and I was frozen in the middle dancing around a decision. Go left and pray he doesn't explode or go right and re-use the dirty nappy. I stared at Jack, willing him to answer me telepathically. He blinked back blankly – damn you, baby boy!

Deep down, motherly instinct suspected that this Chernobyl-level shit was probably the first of many, which meant keeping him commando was not an option. Right it is.

Back inside the dimly lit airport bathroom, I retrieved the destroyed nappy from the bin: *welcome to the end of the line*. 'Jack, this is not going to be fun,' I said, using a paper towel to scrape off the more stubborn stains. 'But just bear with me.'

I rinsed the offending nappy in the sink and held it under the automatic hand dryer. 'See, good as new,' I lied. The minute Jack's soft milky limbs hit the still-wet nappy, he started to scream.

Inside I began to scream, too.

LIFT, MEGAN! Four months ago, you pushed Jack into this world, Megan! You are a majestic giver of life, provider of food and warmth and shelter and milk. You will not be beaten by a dirty, wet nappy. Not today, not tomorrow, not ever! NOW, GET OUT THERE AND GET ON THAT FUCKING PLANE.

We made it back in time to see most passengers obediently boarding the flight, but I couldn't bring myself to join them. Fifteen minutes passed and the crowd thinned until it was just me and my crying boy.

Eventually I heard our names being broadcast across the airwaves by an increasingly impatient blonde flight attendant with an accent, Texan probably.

'This is the final boarding call for passengers Megan and Jack Heywood booked on flight 372A to Tucson, Arizona.'

Please let this next bit go okay.

* * * * * * *

Before I had a child of my own, I used to view plane parents with a mix of sympathy and annoyance. *That must be so difficult,* I would think, plugging my headphones in and browsing the in-flight entertainment. *God, I hope their baby doesn't scream the whole way.*

As the plane took off and Jack did his best to pierce the eardrums of everyone on board, I sent out cosmic apologies to all the parents I had judged in years gone by: *sorry for being a shitty person.*

There were three seats in my row, I took the window, the middle was empty, and my suited friend from the gate had the aisle. I clocked the sheer terror on his face when he realised. Trapped next to the manic mother and her banshee baby.

'Lucky you,' I joked as he squirmed into his seat. 'Let me know if you'd like a hold?'

The second the fasten seat belt sign was switched off, he flagged a flight attendant and asked to move. Who can blame the poor guy – I wish I could've joined him.

After a few minutes, our pilot announced we had reached 'a pleasant cruising altitude', but from where I was sitting, there was nothing pleasant about it. In between blood-curdling cries, Jack's face was twisting and contorting, his legs stiffening and contracting. All warning signs that he was preparing for the second coming; the sequel no one asked for.

'No, no, no, not again, my beautiful boy,' I whispered, but my pleas fell on deaf ears. In my arms I felt his body relax, followed by the familiar whiff of shit wafting under my nose.

'Excuse me,' I said, rushing for the bathroom and squeezing past a couple kissing in the aisle.

'A simple "sorry" would suffice,' replied the girl. What a shame I had left the last of my apologies way back in Los Angeles.

As I locked the door, I recalled how years ago on a flight to Miami, Chris had joked about joining the mile-high club. 'What do you reckon?' he asked, raising an eyebrow. I shut it down. 'No chance: we'd never fit, for starters.'

Of course, there would be no sex of any kind for Chris in the foreseeable future, mile-high or otherwise.

The second rinsing of the nappy was just as traumatic as the first; only this time, I had less space to work with. Plane bathrooms are barely large enough for a single person to manoeuvre in, let alone trying to balance a screaming child while avoiding covering yourself in its shit.

I failed at the last bit actually, noticing a delightful smear of brown on my sleeve as I exited the bathroom. Add it to the list. Back in the seat, Jack was still visibly upset. I had fed him when we first boarded but decided to double down and feed him again. The first rule of new mom club: if in doubt, whip the boob out.

Tried the left boob first, didn't work; right boob next, still no luck. We play this back-and-forth boob game for a few minutes, but nothing does the trick. Jack's hysteria is peaking, so too is mine. I am now nude on a plane full of strangers that hate me.

We must've looked quite heartbreaking because an elderly gentleman soon appeared before us. He was your classic grandad – rounded potbelly, tucked-in polo, smart slacks and comfy shoes.

'Hand me the young lad,' he said softly, looking over the rim of his glasses. Without knowing a single thing about this man, I sensed he could be trusted, so I passed Jack over gently. That's when he began to sing, his voice rusty and deep, in the style of classic crooners. His music seemed to fill the space, and there was no room in the cabin left for anything else. No place for my thoughts, for Jack's crying, for complaints, or drink requests, or anything at all. Just an old man, a young boy and a song.

By the time he finished, Jack was sound asleep. 'Sinatra,' he whispered, handing Jack back to me. 'Works every time with my grandkids.'

If I hadn't been so worried about waking Jack, I would've stood up and planted a kiss on this sensibly dressed baby whisperer. Instead, I settled for a quiet, but heartfelt, 'thank you'.

Minutes later, the plane's mechanics grumbled to life, and I heard the wheels hit the tarmac. We landed with a thud, but Jack didn't bat an eyelid, he was *finally* knocked out.

I still remember that moment perfectly, kissing him on the cheek and stroking his perfect face. 'Sleep well, you little fucker.'

I watched on as people piled off the plane, content just to enjoy the hard-won silence. A few passengers offered me encouraging smiles; I smiled back. We'd survived it together.

Eventually, only the crew remained, so I took that as my cue – but was cut off by a uniformed man with a handlebar moustache. 'Captain Jed Hoover,' he said, sliding into the aisle seat.

Captain Hoover was all testosterone, like a TV pilot but in real life. Few people can pull off a handlebar any more. Captain Hoover was one of them.

'Must admit, that's a first for me,' he explained. 'Ain't it?' The cabin crew nodded in agreement. I was confused.

'I've never heard a baby crying from the cockpit before; this little guy must have a helluva set of lungs on him.'

And with that, Captain Hoover unpinned his pilot wings from above his left shirt pocket. 'Do you mind?' he asked, I shook my head as he carefully fastened them to Jack's little singlet. 'He's earned them and so have you.'

As if that wasn't heroic enough, Captain Hoover then carried my bags off the plane and escorted Jack and me to the arrivals lounge.

'Ummm, who is that dreamy pilot?' asked Aunt Cathy, as Captain Hoover waved us goodbye. I told her he was my new husband.

Under strict instruction, Aunt Cathy had brought a box of fresh nappies to the airport, so she took Jack off my hands and whisked him away for a long-overdue change.

In the distance, I could see my mom deep in conversation with two women I vaguely recognised as being from our hometown. She caught my eye and called me over. 'Megan, you remember Nina and her daughter, Cass?'

I didn't but was too tired to admit the truth. 'Sure, how are you guys? What are you doing here?'

'I'm just here from LA for the weekend,' mumbled Cass. She was your typical valley girl: zero body fat, zero interest.

'And how was your flight?' asked Nina.

'Urgh, you won't even believe it, Mom,' Cass said, scrolling through her phone without bothering to look up. 'This fucking baby screamed the whole time.'

At that exact instant Aunt Cathy returned, holding a freshly changed Jack.

'Wait, you mean this fucking baby?'

****

The baggage carousel goes round and round, thinning out with each loop. Weary travellers are a captive audience, only perking up when they spot their dented suitcase in the line-up.

I stood there for half an hour before realising the conveyor belt was empty. Eventually, a young man pushing a trolley full of trash bags wheeled his way over to me.

'Are you Megan Heywood?' he asked, reading off a clipboard. I felt tense; conversations that started this way never ended well in airports. 'Yes, why?'

'Apologies, Mrs Heywood, but your suitcase got caught on something in the hull of the plane and ripped open, so we had to put all your stuff in trash bags.'

He looked down at the trolley, then back at me. 'We trust the rest of your flight went smoothly.'

THE F*** UP HALL OF FAME

To Pee or Not to Pee

Name: Tycho Brahe   **Rating**: 6/10

Fuck-up: Dying from a burst bladder after refusing to relieve himself during a lavish aristocratic party in 1601.

You know that feeling when you're stuck at a boring dinner party and the host won't stop banging on about how they get their brussels sprouts extra crispy? As the conversation drags on (and on), all you want to do is excuse yourself and make a beeline for the bathroom so you can spend ten minutes scrolling through Instagram. But you can't do that, because it's impolite.

Well, this is the exact situation (minus the Instagram bit) that resulted in the death of sixteenth-century astronomer Tycho Brahe.

If you're not familiar with your sixteenth-century stargazers, Brahe was a pretty big deal, an A-lister of the astronomy scene.

His career highlights include a stint working for the Danish king, discovering a bunch of new stars and also being the first person to prove that comets are objects in space. Brahe was also one of the last naked-eye astronomers, part of an old-school clique who found the advent of the telescope to be an insult.

He was cool, he was mysterious, he was really good at astronomy.

Bottom line: if you were throwing a banquet in 1601 and Brahe wasn't on the guest list, then why even bother having a party?

On one particular evening in 1601, 13 October to be precise, Brahe was invited to a dinner in Prague being hosted by a nobleman. Brahe attended the royal banquet and by all accounts, a riveting time was had by all.

But the thing about banquets is that they tend to go forever and as time ticked on, Brahe was overcome by a quite desperate urge to use the bathroom.

For most people that would be no issue: off you go, don't forget to wash your hands! But as we already know, Brahe was old-school, so a real stickler for politeness and etiquette.

According to his internal moral compass, he believed it was impolite to excuse himself and duck down the hall for sweet relief.

Instead, he battled through the banquet, presumably crossing and recrossing his legs, and nodding at people's tedious anecdotes while imagining what it would be like to unzip and let loose.

Eventually the dinner party came to a close, Brahe rushed home, busted through the front door and rushed to the toilet only to discover his stream was all dried up.

This condition continued for the next week or so. Only occasionally could Brahe muster up a small amount of liquid that escaped his body in painful spurts.

On 24 October, eleven days after the banquet, Brahe's fuck-up proved fatal. He died at home – cause of death: a suspected busted bladder.

Experts have since questioned whether or not a mystery illness may have contributed to Brahe's death, and there was even a theory he might have been poisoned during the banquet!

His body has twice been exhumed, but results remain inconclusive.

One thing is for sure though: Brahe's demise puts paid to the idea that it won't kill you to hold it in. Turns out, it just might.

You Can't Handle the Tooth

Peter's story

The offices of Parks, Owens & Quinn felt exactly like every other law firm I'd visited in the past month. They all seemed to buy the same shitty art to decorate the walls, fit out the lobby with the same cheap leather lounges, and employ the same bored-sounding blonde to work the front desk.

We were all the same too; a bunch of anxious law graduates hoping to be hired as junior solicitors. Following each other around the city, day after day, week after week, job after job.

'Mr Millross? Is there a Mr Millross here?' announced today's secretary.

A few seats down from me a young guy stood up. He was

stuffed uncomfortably into what was clearly a brand-new suit. 'That's me,' he said, unconvincingly.

On closer inspection, everything about this poor guy was new: his suit, his haircut, his briefcase. With an awkward shuffle, he made his way towards the secretary.

'Great, the partners, will see you now,' she replied, showing him through the usual set of double doors.

Once they disappeared, the rest of us began to relax, safe in the knowledge it wasn't our time yet. At thirty-eight, I was the oldest in the line-up by about fifteen years, which made me the odd one out.

Originally I'd been a high school teacher but decided to retrain after life threw a curveball in the form of twins.

My wife and I were living in Greece when we got the news, a doctor changing our lives with four simple words: 'Congratulations, you're having twins!'

We mustn't have reacted in the right way because the doctor pulled hard on his cigarette and exhaled. (It was Greece in the mid-eighties: everyone smoked all the time, even doctors.)

'You're not happy?'

Louise and I looked at each other, were we happy? She put two hands on her belly, one for each of the babies. The questions piled up inside my head: how the fuck will we afford it? Would they be identical? Do we *have* to dress them the same?

The doctor took a seat. 'You know in Greece, we have a saying: *Είναι γλυκό να βλέπεις τη θάλασσα, όταν στέκεται στην ακτή* – "it's sweet to view the sea when standing on the shore".'

I waited for an explanation. Being Greek myself, I knew the only thing we love more than proverbs is explaining what they mean. And sure enough, he continued: 'What this means is that once a struggle has passed, you won't look back at it and feel such pain. Bad times pass, good times endure.' He smiled, as if that settled it.

Thanks for your thoughts, doc, but I had a proverb of my own: *twins: fuck me, that sounds expensive.*

The impending arrival of double trouble had a domino effect. We left Greece and moved home to Australia. I quit teaching and started studying law while working two jobs to support the family: one early in the morning, one late at night.

Six years and two kids later and here I was, the most senior of wannabe junior solicitors.

'Are you nervous?' asked the girl sitting next to me, ripping me back into reality, back into the Parks, Owens & Quinn pressure cooker.

'A little, yeah,' I replied. I didn't know her name but recognised the face. Like all the others she was young, no more than twenty-five.

'Me too,' she said, pausing to think. 'But you must have loads of life experience though!'

I laughed, and she joined in, but not for the same reason. At first I'd fooled myself into thinking life experience would work in my favour, but so far the novelty of a near-forty-year-old applicant hadn't paid off.

Younger graduates could work longer hours for less money and not worry about feeding a family. Speaking of hungry families, Louise had recently fallen pregnant again – not twins, thank God – but another child meant my balls were getting busted harder than ever.

Suddenly our two-bedroom house was too cramped; the car was too small, and we needed a backyard that was bigger than a postage stamp.

Usually Louise was patient, but my spell of thanks-but-no-thanks job interviews was doing her head in. She would never say it, but I could tell what she was thinking. *What's the point of rolling the dice and retraining, if no one will hire you?*

The more I thought about it, the more obvious it seemed: I wasn't just nervous; I was desperate.

At that moment, the double doors swung open, and the receptionist reappeared followed by a defeated-looking Millross. 'We'll be in touch,' she said, but they wouldn't be. She scanned her clipboard and stepped forward. 'Is there a Mr Conomos here?'

The girl next to me caught my eye and mouthed 'good luck'. Then I picked up my empty briefcase and walked towards the blonde.

'The partners will see you now.'

****

Twenty-four hours earlier

'Does this look normal to you?'

In the mirror, Dennis watched on as I wiggled my front tooth back and forth with my tongue. He shook his head.

'Of course, it doesn't,' I continued. 'Because you fucked it up!'

We were sitting in Dennis's clinic, which was really just his living room with a dental chair in the corner. There were religious icons all over the joint which to me sent the wrong message. *Time for your root canal, let's pray it goes well!*

'Peter, I'm sorry, you know I'm still learning,' said Dennis, leaning back against a picture of a disappointed Jesus. He seemed oblivious to the fact that, as a dentist, this isn't something you should admit out loud.

'Let me fix it,' he offered, patting the chair and beckoning me over. 'You know I love you like a brother!'

I didn't love Dennis like a brother, I loved him like a second cousin – because that's exactly what he was. And that was the only reason I let him anywhere near my mouth. That's how it works with the Greeks. If your uncle's a mechanic, he fixes your car. If your sister's husband has a fruit shop, that's where you go to buy oranges.

And unfortunately, if your second cousin is a clueless dentist whose makeshift clinic feels more like an Orthodox church, then he 'fixes' your teeth.

While Louise refused to let Dennis treat the kids, I had no choice. Every time I threatened to go to someone else, Dennis would tell *his* mother, who would phone *my* mother, who would then call me.

'PETER! PETER!' My mother was unable to start a sentence without yelling my name at least twice. 'Dennis's mother told me you want a new dentist? I grew up with her in the *village*!'

She added a little spice to the word 'village' just so I understood how long they'd known each other.

'I know that, Mum,' I replied. 'But he's no good!'

'PETER! PETER! How your cousin get better if you don't heeeeelp him? Είναι αίμα, Είναι οικογένεια! He is *blood*, he is *family*!'

'But is he actually a dentist?'

And with that the conversation was over, the Greek guilt trip in full force. In the last couple of months, I'd developed an ache in my front tooth and begrudgingly gone to see Dennis about it.

'That looks like –' he paused and scanned through a book, flipping pages in a hurry '– an abscess!'

I'll never know if he was right, but either way Dennis pulled the tooth out and whacked a false one in. Over the past few weeks the tooth had refused to stay in place, constantly feeling like it was going to drop out.

Now that I had the interview lined up, I couldn't risk any fuck-ups, so here I was, back for another round of experimental treatment.

'I can use a little dental cement to keep it in place, but you have to be careful,' warned Dennis. 'It needs time to settle, so avoid alcohol and hot drinks like coffee or tea because they will soften the cement.'

Whatever you say, cousin.

* * * * * *

'Coffee before we begin, Mr Conomos?'

The blonde was mid-pour when she asked the question, so I didn't have much choice.

'That would be great, thank you.' The three partners all nodded in agreement and it seemed I'd passed the first test, accepting their offer of instant coffee.

They sat on the opposite side of a long boardroom table, Parks in the middle, flanked by Owens and Quinn. The gap between us was just that little bit too big, meaning whenever someone spoke, I had to lean forward to hear what was said.

'Conomos, is that Greek?' asked Parks, kicking things off with a bit of nationality small talk.

'It is,' I confirmed, pretending to sip my coffee.

'I knew it! My sister's husband, Jim, is Greek,' she said, smiling at the coincidence.

There were over a hundred thousand Greeks living in Australia in 1994, but I got the feeling Parks expected me to know exactly who she was talking about: *Jim, of course, I'll say hello to him at the next club meeting!*

'There are plenty of us, but only one of me,' I said, hoping to steer the conversation back towards my main goal: selling myself.

My segue had the desired effect. Smiles all round and we quickly slipped into official interview territory. For the next ten minutes, Parks, Owens & Quinn took turns firing questions my way.

It was all familiar stuff: *tell us about yourself, what are your strengths and weaknesses*, that kind of thing. By the time I got through explaining where I saw myself in five years, they were lapping it up.

'You certainly would be an asset to any firm, Peter,' said Parks.

'Very impressive,' agreed Quinn, clearing his throat then leaning over to whisper in the ear of Parks.

Here we go, I thought, here comes the curve ball. In every panel interview there's always one person who tries to trip you up with a surprise question. Knock you off balance and see what happens.

'So explain to me, Peter,' he started, tapping his fingers on the table. 'Why should we hire you, and not those young guns?' Game time. If I was going to clinch it, I had to nail this next bit.

'That's a great question, Mr Quinn.' Flattery first, a crucial building block of any big speech. 'You know, I've done this a few times now, and with each knockback I've had to ask myself: *Have I left it too late?*'

We all considered this hypothetical question as the secretary appeared with a pot of fresh coffee, she topped us all up and then Parks gestured at me to continue.

'But while some firms have seen my age as a weakness, I see it as a secret weapon.'

Enthusiastic nodding from the panel, that's an encouraging sign, everyone loves an underdog.

'The difference between me and those *kids* ... it's more than just age, it's maturity. Sure, we all graduated from law school, but how many of them have graduated from the university of life?'

Owens seemed to like that one, he beamed across the table and offered a thumbs up. *Keep going, Peter.* 'Born in Greece, I moved here with my parents as a young boy . . .'

That's it, play the plucky immigrant card. This is good stuff.

'. . . Since then I've travelled the world, living and working in three different countries, learning four different languages. During that time, I've come to understand that empathy is our most potent currency.'

Most potent. Even I couldn't believe my own bullshit.

'The ability to look someone in the eye and understand their struggle will always be far more valuable than –' strategic stop to glance towards the doors to the lobby, where the baby-faced competition waited patiently for their shot '– having time on your side.'

The three partners exchanged a look that said, 'He's good, he's good!' In hindsight, I should've just shut the fuck up at that point, but I was on a roll.

'Finally, I know this is a family firm with family values and as the father of twins with another one on the way –' one final pause to allow the number of my dependants to sink in '– working hard for them means working hard for you – and *that's* why you should hire me, and not those young guys.'

I looked directly at Quinn as I delivered this last line. He smiled back at me and clasped his hands. Not quite a standing ovation but the best you're gonna get from a partner.

Once I finished my one-man show they started talking among themselves, commenting to each other about the points I'd made. It's human nature to distract yourself in a moment like that, so you reach for something, anything. *The coffee.*

Without thinking, I picked up the cup and took a luxurious victory sip, forgetting about the false fuckin' tooth that was temporarily cemented into my head.

The second it touched my lips I felt a bolt of pain shoot through my gums – but that was nothing compared with what I heard when I placed the mug back on the table. PLOP.

The scalding caffeine must've melted the cement, dislodging the tooth, and the false fucker was already airborne. In absolute horror I watched as my incisor dropped out of my mouth and landed square in the coffee cup.

The tooth broke the surface with force, causing a mushroom cloud of splashback, kind of like when the military detonates underwater bombs at sea. KABOOM!

Forget storm in a teacup; this was a shitshow in a coffee mug.

Dennis, you're a dead man! I was thinking about all the ways I would hurt my second cousin when Parks turned her attention to me.

'That was some answer, Peter,' she said, leaning back in her chair. I responded with a drawn out mmmm – my only option at this point. 'You really want this don't you?' she continued.

'Mm-hmm!' I agreed, trying to muster as much enthusiasm as possible through a closed mouth.

'And do you have any questions?' asked Parks.

'Mmm?' My upward inflection must've given the impression I was unfamiliar with the concept of questioning because Parks looked stumped.

'Uh, do you have any questions ... for us ... regarding the role?'

'Mm-mm,' I responded, slowly twisting my head from side to side like an amusement park clown.

Having survived the *mmmm-m*inefield, the interview finally wrapped up and talk turned to more general matters, Parks and Quinn discussing recent changes to precedent in the Supreme Court. Every so often I chipped in with another *Mmmm*, as if I was constantly mulling everything over.

Internally, my panic centred around one thing: *how to get the tooth*. I needed to take it with me, one way or another. Even with the family discount, Dennis had charged me a couple of grand for the false tooth and I didn't have that kind of cash lying around.

The sensible move was to tell the partners what had happened and hope they saw the funny side. But the stakes were too high: outside the office were ten young solicitors with full sets of teeth waiting for me to slip up.

The panicked option was to drain the coffee, swallow my tooth and then figure the fucking rest out later – which is exactly what I did.

Finishing the meeting basically mute, I shook hands with the partners and left in a hurry, destination: Dennis the dentist.

His clinic was a fifteen-minute drive from the office. I made it in ten, banging on the front door in desperation. 'Dennis, I swallowed the false tooth. Let me in!'

Finally he opened the door, looking half-asleep. In his defence it was midday on a Monday so he was probably busy doing fuck-all. 'Peter, what happened? The cement didn't hold?'

I came clean, admitting to my accidental victory sip, Dennis threw his hands up in frustration. 'What did I tell you? You'll have to just go through the motions,' he said, eyes drifting to my stomach.

Um, motions?

'Literally. Should only take a couple of days to pass, then once it does, we can give it a clean and I'll put it back in.'

As far as falls from grace are concerned, this was a pretty dramatic one. In the space of a few hours I'd gone from promising junior solicitor to contemplating a search-and-rescue mission in my own shit.

I said goodbye to Dennis through gritted teeth – what was left of them – then spent the rest of the afternoon at the library scanning the paper for job ads before finally heading home. Tail between my legs, tooth in my stomach.

'Sounds like the interview went well,' Louise yelled as I walked through the door.

'What do you mean?' I asked, dumping my briefcase.

'Check the answering machine.' I pressed play and Parks' voice filled the room.

'Mr Conomos, it's Elaine Parks here. Thank you so much for coming in today. The partners were very impressed with you and we'd love to have a follow-up – I trust Wednesday morning works. See you then.' BEEP.

Wednesday morning. It was Monday evening.

Louise came into the living room and gave me a one-sided hug. 'That's great news, why do you look so sad?'

I smiled, revealing my toothless grin in all its glory. She didn't even try to stop the laughter.

* * * * * * *

'ANOTHER ONE, QUICK!'

Rock bottom is hollering at your pregnant wife to fetch another bucket, because the one you're sitting on is full. 'HURRY!'

Louise tossed me the bucket while trying (and failing) to keep the kids inside so they weren't scarred for life. I heard the back door open and locked eyes with my son. 'Dad, what are you doing?'

DON'T LOOK AT ME, BOY!

With the clock ticking to retrieve the tooth, Louise had come up with the genius idea of using over-the-counter laxatives as a way of speeding things up.

'Go to the supermarket, stock up on whatever you can buy and then just let nature take its course. Just *go with the flow*!' She was enjoying this too much.

I had no choice but to follow her advice, which explains why I was glued to a bucket in the backyard.

Each hour followed the same disgusting routine. A tell-tale rumble in my stomach signalled the start of an aggressive bowel movement. Once that was over, I would sift through my shit, using a flashlight to try and catch a glimpse of anything resembling a tooth. Like finding a needle in a haystack, except *way* worse.

This was the cycle I was trapped in until Tuesday night around 9 pm, when I felt the rumble once more. Lo and behold, amid the waste, there it was: my missing incisor. 'Louise! Come quick!'

She came crashing through the back door and together we gazed upon this hideous trophy in delight. Somewhere in my mind I heard the soft lapping of waves and the faint echo of these words: *It's sweet to view the sea when standing on the shore.*

After all these years, they finally made sense.

* * * * * * *

After the bucket ordeal, I rushed the tooth to Dennis and made sure he put that false fucker in nice and tight. The next day, none the wiser, Parks, Owens & Quinn hired me on the spot.

Three weeks into my time there, Parks – or Elaine as I now called her – stopped by my desk.

'Peter, just a little something from the partners to say welcome to the Parks, Owens & Quinn family,' she said, handing me a package.

I unwrapped the box and pulled out a personalised mug that read: *You can't handle the tooth!*

My hand subconsciously reached for my mouth, my face a mix of disbelief and confusion.

'Wait, what . . . but how?'

Elaine laughed and picked up the mug. 'Didn't I tell you my sister's husband, Jim, is Greek?'

I nodded.

'Well, guess who his dentist is?'

THE F*** UP HALL OF FAME

Loyal to a Fault

> **Name**: Second Lieutenant Hiroo Onoda   **Rating**: 29/10
>
> **Fuck-up**: Refusing to believe Japan had surrendered World War II in 1945, Second Lieutenant Hiroo Onoda fought on for another twenty-nine years. He finally called it a day in 1974.

If you've ever rolled your eyes when your manager has asked you to work late, then spare a thought for Hiroo Onoda – the Japanese soldier who accidentally did three decades of overtime.

Onoda was a second lieutenant in the Japanese Imperial Army during World War II. On 26 December 1944, he was shipped off to Lubang Island in the Philippines by his commanding officer, Major Yoshimi Taniguchi.

At the time, Japan was on the brink of defeat, but Taniguchi's final orders were crystal clear: stay! fight! never surrender!

Of course, this is classic military bravado, and while you should 'never surrender', Taniguchi probably didn't expect

Onoda to take the orders *so* literally. It's kind of like when your high school football coach tells you to *never give up!* But really, you're allowed to give up. No one will mind.

Shortly after landing, the Allies overpowered the Japanese Army, wiping out pretty much everyone except for Onoda and three other officers, who escaped into the jungle.

Fast forward to 15 August 1945: Japan officially surrendered, bringing an end to the Second World War. Everyone was overjoyed, except for Onoda and his motley crew who continued to fight a non-existent battle against a phantom enemy.

Over the next *twenty-nine* years, there were several unsuccessful attempts to coax the men out of hiding. In October 1945, leaflets were dropped into the jungle explaining Japan had surrendered. Onoda didn't buy it.

In 1952, the Japanese Army tried a personal touch, dropping family photos and handwritten letters. Onoda doubled down: this was nothing more than propaganda.

Over time, Onoda's group of four dwindled. Two men were killed in shootouts with villagers; another simply gave up – but not Onoda.

By 1972, he was the last man standing, but it wasn't until two years later, in 1974, that Norio Suzuki, a Japanese student, discovered him.

Suzuki had travelled to Lubang specifically to look for Onoda. The pair became friendly, but even with hard proof from Suzuki that the war was over (and had been for twenty-nine years), Onoda refused to give in.

He explained to Suzuki that he had strict orders from Major Taniguchi, and until he heard otherwise, Onoda wasn't going anywhere. Talk about dedication.

This forced the Japanese government to track down Taniguchi, who had done a serious lane change and was now running a charming bookshop in a small town, and fly him out to Lubang Island to relieve Onoda of his duties.

On 9 March 1974, nearly thirty years since the two men had laid eyes on one another, Taniguchi finally met with Onoda and ordered him to stand down.

At fifty-two, Onoda returned to Japan a national hero and promptly turned his fuck-up into a money-making opportunity, receiving a handsome sum for his biography, *No Surrender: My Thirty-Year War*.

All I Want For Christmas Is a Do-Over

Sarah's story

All my life I'd been the kind of girl who played by the rules. Not because I was told to, but because I got a thrill out of doing the right thing.

At school, assignments were handed in on time – or early – and I knew boundaries were there for a reason, to be respected not pushed. I was a model teenager, who was also in the Model United Nations.

'Why can't you be more like Sarah?' was a common phrase among my friends' parents. They would invite me over for dinner and smile as I cleared my own dishes and thanked them for a lovely meal. 'Such nice manners, too! Are you sure we can't keep you?'

They would laugh and I would laugh, mostly because I knew the deal would never fly with my parents. They were both teachers at the same school, which also happened to be my school.

Most days it felt like class started when you woke up, and didn't stop until you fell asleep, not that my sister and I were bothered. We were independently studious; we never argued over the TV remote in our house, because the TV was rarely switched on.

Instead, free time was spent reading, curling up in individual corners of the house to absorb whatever we could. Mum would float from room to room offering cups of tea, maybe an Arnott's biscuit.

After graduating school I watched, more curious than envious, as my girlfriends splintered off to explore and experiment. Stories of gap years and good times would trickle back, and I would ask the right questions and feign jealousy – 'send more pics!' – but I was completely content.

I had always seen education as a wholly linear experience, no time to waste, so I threw myself into a law degree. Unsurprisingly, my parents were totally supportive, imploring me to stay at home while I studied.

'We can even turn Gemma's old room into a study,' suggested Mum. 'It gets such nice light in the afternoon.'

My older sister had moved out a couple of years earlier, taking a job with a not-for-profit on the south coast, while working on her thesis. She still drove back every Sunday for family lunch, wowing us with tales of her exciting new life away from the family bubble.

It was during this time that Gemma met Scott, an artist who lived and worked in his studio.

I immediately liked Scott: he wasn't bothered about history, didn't care for facts and figures. Coming from a family that held impromptu history quizzes over dinner, Scott was refreshing. But for these same reasons my parents were wary, often referring to him as a 'phase'.

'Did you see his face when I mentioned the Battle of Verdun? Completely blank,' muttered Dad one night after dinner. 'Don't worry, Craig, I'm sure it's just a *phase*,' Mum would reply.

When Gemma fell pregnant unexpectedly, it was the first time that things hadn't really gone to plan for our family. No one wanted to admit it, or say it out loud, but it was true. She was twenty-three and had only been with Scott for a few months and now they were having a baby.

It wasn't like it was bad news or anything, just a shock. Well, at least that's how Mum sold it to her friends. 'Craig and I are really very excited,' she'd say, nodding too much. 'It's just a bit of shock, you know?'

Once the dust settled, Mum, Dad and I went about our lives and, to the naked eye, everything seemed normal. But if you knew what to look for, it was clear something had changed. As if we had been spinning perfectly on an axis, and Gemma's announcement had caused the slightest, almost imperceptible, wobble. Yet it was still a wobble.

Shortly after the baby news my famously frugal parents decided to gift themselves an early Christmas present: an extravagant outdoor spa. It was December 2016.

* * * * * * *

'I reckon we get the Gemini 2000,' declared Dad, thumbing through brochures over breakfast. 'The Mercury plunge pool has more jets, but the Gemini fits five comfortably.'

Like most dads, mine refused to commit to any serious purchase without weeks of intense research. There would be no parting with his 'hard-earned' until he had scoured the spa market for all available options.

Eventually, they did settle on the Gemini 2000, a garish mix of faux wood panelling and jet-black plastic. From what I'd seen, spas are never subtle in design, but this was particularly hideous.

For a while, it was all my parents could talk about.

'Imagine being able to have a spa every night of the week,'

my mother would say, as if this were the missing piece of the puzzle. 'I'll be a different person!'

Final installation took place three days before Christmas. After it was finished the three of us hovered awkwardly in our swimming costumes, waiting for the water to heat up.

'Beautiful isn't it, and your father managed to wrangle free delivery *and* setup,' Mum said proudly, dipping a hand in to check the temperature. 'It will add *so* much value when we sell!'

While I questioned how many prospective buyers saw an outdoor spa and thought, 'This place is worth double what we offered!' I kept my mouth shut. Truth is I was just as excited as my parents were. University was finished for the semester, but I'd enrolled in a summer research program which started in the new year. Considering I was about to spend my entire holiday reading up on the ethical basis of trademark law and how it informs the complex world of intellectual property, it might as well be in a spa.

With the Gemini 2000 officially a permanent fixture in our backyard it was time to celebrate. I grabbed a bottle of champagne and a few glasses.

'Let's send Gemma a pic,' said Dad, so we all crowded into our new spa and grinned stupidly for a selfie. 'Bub and I can't wait!' came the reply, alongside a photo of Gemma cradling her belly.

'You, me, Mum, Gemma and the baby.' Dad counted on his fingers. 'Lucky it fits five comfortably!' Semi-submerged and wonderfully warm, I popped the champagne and proposed a toast.

'To the Gemini 2000,' I laughed, while clinking their glasses. 'I never wanted a spa until we got one!'

'Oh Sarah, can you please use those special plastic cups I bought,' answered Mum, adjusting her costume and taking a sip. 'No glass in the spa, okay? Come on, you know better than that.'

****

Christmas Eve

'Are you sure your parents won't mind?' asked my friend Minna from the front seat of the cab, the red lights of the meter dancing across her face.

'No, they're cool,' I said casually, but I could feel Andrew looking at me. We'd been close since forever and he knew as well as I did that my parents weren't cool. Not being cool was a label they wore proudly – and one I'd inherited.

Annoyingly, Andrew was cool because he was in a band and when you're twenty-one, that's all it takes.

We had spent the night watching them play at a local pub. I wanted to be cool-by-association, which meant tagging along to all their gigs, even on Christmas Eve.

'Andrew is gorgeous,' Minna shouted in my ear, as the guys on stage screeched through a song that sounded much like all their others. 'He could be my Christmas present!'

While Andrew had the mysterious muso thing going on, he was like a brother to me and the idea of anyone sleeping with him made me shudder. The same couldn't be said for Justin though, the band's doe-eyed drummer.

We'd been on a couple of dates a few years ago. Actually, they were more like trial dates; coffee in the afternoon kind of thing, a fact-finding mission. There was definite chemistry but then he moved overseas and the whole thing fizzled out. Now Justin was back and as he whacked away at the drums, it was hard not to see him as unfinished business.

'Justin's gorgeous too,' added Minna, confirming what I was already thinking. 'We should all hang out after they wrap up!'

The band returned for a Christmas-themed encore, delighting the crowd with a punk cover of 'Rudolph the Red-nosed Reindeer'.

As the song finished, Justin gave me a wink and I was overtaken by the panic that this magical night – with all its promise – would come to an end. I was in no rush to arrive at what came next: *Gemma's baby; summer university; reading, reading and more reading.*

And so, drunk on festivity (and several bottles of white wine) I rolled the dice. 'Why doesn't everyone come back to mine to kick on?' The crowd of people around me voiced their approval, chants of 'kick on, kick on' boosting my confidence. 'We even have a spa!'

Back in the cab, the familiar twists and turns told me we were almost home.

'So, you said you've got a spa?' said Justin, brushing his long hair out of his stupidly pretty face.

'Yeah we do, a Gemini 2000,' I replied, catching his eye in the rear-view mirror. He smiled.

****

By the time we arrived at my parents' place, there was already a group waiting out the front. I recognised most faces, but not all, and safely filed this thought away under 'things I will worry about tomorrow'.

'Do you mind if I tell a few more people to meet us here?' asked Justin as we climbed out of the car. 'You said your parents were cool?'

The correct answer was: Look Justin, I've already over-extended myself and if I'm being totally honest, my parents don't even like hosting people they know. In fact, the only reason I'm throwing this spontaneous shindig is to get you into bed, so why don't we send everyone else home, then you and I can have a spa-rty for two?

Ignoring my inner voice, I said: 'Definitely! Do you need the address?'

Oh, Little Drummer Boy, how can I let you down?

I was well and truly panicking now, and I knew the only way forward was to ply myself with more booze.

Another rite of passage when hosting a house party against your parents' wishes is to raid their alcohol supply. Dad kept cases of beer stacked in the garage, but I had always been more impressed by his dusty collection of red wine. Figuring my guests would appreciate something a little fancy, I stacked the bottles on the kitchen counter.

'Drink up everyone!' I yelled, wondering who I was and why I was saying these things. I spied two empty wine bottles near the sink, no doubt polished off by my parents earlier that night. *Please let that be enough to keep them asleep.* Their bedroom was on the third floor, separated from the rest of the house by a long corridor. Dad was a deep sleeper and Mum used ear plugs at night, so with a little luck they wouldn't stir.

Snaking through the living room I tried to ignore the people using books as coasters – a crime punishable by death in our family – and focused my energies on Justin. He was huddled in the corner, drinking a sickeningly expensive Malbec out of a mug that read BEST MUM EVER.

'Should we fire it up?' he said, handing me the mug and turning towards the spa. Looking back, this was another fork in the road: say no and the sanctity of the spa remains intact. Say yes, and whatever happens, happens.

I drained what was left in the cup and headed outside.

****

Justin made a beeline for the spa, and was quickly joined by Andrew, Minna and our other friend, Ally. I jumped in and was delighted to realise the five of us, wearing nothing but our undies, did fit comfortably – just as the Gemini 2000 promised. Dad would be happy about that, if nothing else.

Between the bubbles and booze, I finally began to relax. Visions of my parents waking up to discover a Christmas Eve festival in the backyard faded from view. I was certain there would be a price to pay, but it really is difficult to worry when you're in a spa, even with Ally poking me in the ribs.

She was drawing my attention to Andrew and Minna, who were kissing so violently they appeared to be inhaling one another. I was unmoved by the sudden spa smooch, aware that the combination of high-powered jets and warm water could be an aphrodisiac. Terrifyingly, it had been a hot topic between my parents during the spa's installation.

'Pretty sexy don't you reckon, Carol?' Dad had said, slowly caressing the plastic and robbing me of any future orgasms. 'Shall I turn the jets on?'

But now that the jets were on, I could see he had a point: pretty sexy indeed. What happened next, I can only put down to the mystical power of the spa. Justin floated over to me and taking a cue from Andrew and Minna, planted a years-in-the-making kiss on my lips.

Ally sharply read the room and excused herself, muttering something about a late-night snack.

As she slipped away, tiptoeing off to bed, a remaining sober pocket of my brain recognised the exit to be a smart move, especially since things were lifting off in the spa.

At some point, Andrew and Minna had removed their underwear and were edging closer to starring in their very own soft porn film. While I'd already crossed several boundaries, engaging in a public sex act in my parents' three-day-old spa was a stretch. Time to hit eject.

'I need to use the bathroom.' Pulling away from Justin, I directed my eyes towards the house. We dried off and left Andrew and Minna to their jet-fuelled romp.

'Can't believe they're about to christen the spa,' said Justin, his voice muffled from the other side of the door. I was sitting upstairs in 'the nice bathroom', typically reserved for guests. It had a clear view down to the backyard where the party was finally thinning out.

'Or maybe your parents got there first, sexy spa times for Mum and Dad.'

Looking in the mirror, I decided I would still have sex with me, so it was time to seal the deal. I opened the door to see Justin leaning against a bookshelf, flicking through a book.

I desperately hoped he wouldn't turn around to see several framed photos of Gemma and me from our awkward teen years. Why had we done so much karate, and why had it been so extensively photographed?

'It's funny, actually: your dad and I have loads of the same books; we must have really similar taste.'

'Please stop talking about my dad, Justin,' I said, taking a step towards him and removing the book from his delightful drummer hands. 'Actually, let's stop talking altogether.'

As we kissed, I heard the clock downstairs chime, it was just after midnight. Merry Christmas to me.

* * * * * * *

When you're young, Christmas Day is one of the few days on the calendar that you can't get in trouble for waking up early.

Most kids toss and turn through the night, too excited to sleep. By the time the light creeps in, they're up and ready while exhausted parents hover near the kettle trying to muster up some enthusiasm. But in our house, everything operated in reverse.

At 6 am, Dad would bound in, shake us awake, the stench of freshly peeled prawns already clinging to his hands.

'Who's up for a family photo?' No one was interested, but we would begrudgingly take part.

Besides Grand Final day, Christmas was Dad's absolute favourite time of the year, so we didn't want to disappoint. Come 7 am, he was in the kitchen cooking breakfast, Michael Bublé crooning in the background.

He followed this routine every year without fail, so when I checked my phone and saw it was 7.15 am, a nervous chill shuddered through my body: *Dad must be awake.*

Desperate to offload my anxiety onto someone else, I rolled over to wake Justin, but he was dead to the world. In the harsh light of day, he had far more tattoos than I first realised. I noticed a smiley face that stretched out across his lower back. *What are you smiling at exactly?*

I decided to commit Justin's entire inked body to memory as a way of avoiding going downstairs. Halfway down his left arm I heard screams followed by the crash of the front door.

'ON BLOODY CHRISTMAS MORNING!' Dad's voice thundered through the house as clothing started sailing across the front yard. First, a pair of pants.

Outside my window I spied a naked Andrew and Minna hightailing it up the street. This was bad news.

'HAVE SOME RESPECT!' Next came Minna's dress.
'THE HOLIEST OF DAYS!' A single shoe.
'WHEN JESUS DIED ON THE CROSS!' And the other shoe.

We're not really religious, so forgive the mix-up but Dad had other things on his mind.

Turns out he had waltzed downstairs full of festive cheer only to be greeted by the sight of Minna and Andrew going at it under the kitchen table. Now I wasn't there, but I've heard Dad tell the story that many times, I can almost quote him verbatim: 'Picture this! You go downstairs for a cuppa on Christmas morning and you're greeted by some bloke's bare arse. Christ Almighty! Pretty sad looking arse too, if I'm honest.

'I must've ruined the mood, my sincerest apologies ha-ha, because he's stopped mid-pump, so now I'm looking at his jingle balls dangling in the air. Jingle balls! Ha-ha!

'But seriously, what a disgrace! I blew my top and they quickly made themselves pretty scarce, didn't even bother collecting their clothes, did a nude runner out the front door.

'Honestly, you wouldn't read about it.'

Cue Dad's front lawn meltdown, and my realisation that it was time to face the music. I left a sleeping Justin in the bed and crept downstairs. 'Dad,' I said sheepishly.

He was sitting in the kitchen, head in his hands, surrounded by bottles, a bowl of prawns waiting patiently to be peeled.

At that same moment, the screen door slid open and a man I'd never seen before entered the kitchen from the backyard. 'Thanks for having us, Sarah,' the stranger said casually.

No worries at all. Also: who are you?

In silence, we watched him walk out the front door then Dad and I turned our attention to where he'd come from: the backyard. A scene far more confronting than Andrew's nude peach.

The trees were full of clothes, the grass ground down to mud and someone had knocked over our 'Santa please stop here!' sign.

Admittedly, there was a lot to be angry about, but Dad only had eyes for the spa. He wrestled the lid off and we both stepped back. Way worse than I could have imagined.

Cigarette butts clung to the side of the spa, there was broken glass everywhere and floating in the middle, an enormous turd. The once pristine Gemini 2000 now a soupy brown slosh pit.

'God, I hope that's dog shit,' sighed Dad, which I thought was remarkably optimistic, especially since we don't own a dog.

It was around this time my dad should've self-combusted but instead he just stared silently into the abyss that was the Gemini 2000. Rather than disturb whatever quiet breakdown he was experiencing, I decided to start cleaning, piling up bottles and keeping the clinking to a minimum so as not to alert the neighbours.

'CRAIG, COME QUICK!' yelled Mum from the kitchen, shattering the silence and waking up the greater metropolitan area.

Dad snapped out of his brown funk and ran for the door, me tailing close behind. As soon as we made it inside, my stomach dropped. The fridge door was ajar, I could see an empty space where the Christmas ham was supposed to be.

Dad's face cracked. He'd kept his cool through so much that morning: sex in the kitchen, a stranger in the backyard, 'dog' shit in the spa. This proved a blow too many.

'My ham!'

Justin appeared in the kitchen, and disappeared just as quickly, the look on Dad's face enough to send him bolting. Right after his exit, we heard more footsteps and Ally, who at this point had been asleep for nearly twelve hours, made her triumphant return.

She'd worn my pyjamas to bed, but they were barely recognisable, the front of her shirt covered in what looked like blood. 'What's all over your shirt?' I asked.

'Maple honey glaze,' deadpanned my dad, answering for her. 'It's maple honey glaze with mustard.'

****

It should come as no surprise that Christmas Day was tense that year. I spent every dollar in my bank account replacing the alcohol I'd generously given out.

In the week that followed, each of my friends stopped by and offered their apologies. Some brought wine, others brought chocolates. Justin delivered a stack of books by an author that he and Dad both like. Minna sent flowers but didn't come in; I guess she figured Dad had seen enough of her for a little while.

With each visit my parents softened and before long they softened towards me too. Dad sat me down and offered an olive branch in the shape of a book titled *Rebellious Daughters*.

'Pretty fitting, don't you reckon?'

I'm still banned from using the spa but I'm not that fussed. These days it's full of infant piss from Hadley. Oh yeah: Gemma had the baby, a little girl called Hadley.

Every Sunday we have family spa day, though I just sit back and watch as Mum, Dad, Gemma, Scott and Hadley splash in the water. The Gemini 2000 fits five comfortably.

THE F*** UP HALL OF FAME

Hard Act to Follow

> **Name**: Emperor Shah Jahan   **Rating**: 8/10
>
> **Fuck-up**: Experimenting with an ancient aphrodisiac which would prove nearly fatal, sparking a bloody war for the throne and eventually leading to the fall of the Mughal Empire.

Regularly held up as the crème de la crème of doting husbands, Emperor Shah Jahan is most famous for constructing India's picture-perfect tourist magnet, the Taj Mahal.

Commissioned in 1632 and completed in 1648, the Taj was built in honour of the emperor's dearly departed wife, Mumtaz Mahal, and has since become an international icon for immortal love.

Each year millions of people flock to Agra, India, to see the Taj in the flesh. Lured by the heartwarming tale of an emperor so rocked by his wife's death that he spent the modern equivalent of a billion dollars constructing a magnificent tomb for her.

Obviously, the Taj has worked wonders for the emperor's reputation, the all-marble monument a testament to his everlasting devastation.

But everlasting devastation can only last so long and by 1657 Shah Jahan was starting to feel a little frisky. Mumtaz had been dead for more than twenty years and the emperor's eye began to wander.

Rumour has it Shah Jahan kept several women in the court but had become especially enamoured with a young Moorish slave. Despite his desire, the emperor found himself betrayed by an ageing body: at sixty-five, things just weren't working the way they once did.

Rather than accept that old age had dimmed his voracious sexual appetite the emperor decided to wind back the clock, employing the finest medical men from across the land to administer a cocktail of aphrodisiacs and stimulants.

The treatment was a dismal failure and instead of re-capturing his youth, the reverse occurred. Experimenting with this seventeenth-century version of Viagra left the emperor crippled, weak and suffering from painful bouts of urinary retention.

By 6 September 1657, a gravely ill Emperor Shah Jahan appeared to be at death's door. News of his ill health spread around the empire, spurring his four sons, each believing he deserved the throne, into action – cue, a bloody and brutal sibling war, resulting in thousands of unnecessary deaths.

Eventually, Aurangzeb, the third son and sixth child of the emperor, emerged victorious, having slaughtered two of his brothers on his way to the throne.

All this because Shah Jahan wasn't *down* with not being able to get it *up*.

To make Shah Jahan's story even more outrageous, he didn't even end up dying! The old boy bounced back from his accidental aphrodisiac overdose and lived for another six years. Admittedly, they weren't the smoothest six years: he was imprisoned by Aurangzeb in Agra Fort from July 1658 until his death in January 1666, aged 74. But as far as fuck-ups go, it is the historical footnote to this tale that genuinely makes it legendary.

It's commonly accepted that Aurangzeb's forty-nine-year reign on the throne was disastrous. While he rapidly expanded the Mughal Empire, his brutality is widely blamed for destroying the empire and precipitating the start of British colonialism.

The fall of an empire traced back to Emperor Shah Jahan's desire for one final rise.

The Art of Disappointing Your Parents

Matthew's story

The best thing about being a constant disappointment to your parents is that it sets a low bar.

The more you let them down, the less they expect of you, and that means when you do something good, or even just something regular, they'll lose their shit.

On my twenty-second birthday, I awoke to my parents standing in my bedroom door, singing 'Happy Birthday' at the top of their lungs.

Mum had baked a strawberry cheesecake, my favourite, which was sweating under the blaze of twenty-two candles. Even my dad, who hated birthdays, and singing, and mornings, looked stoked. This was them losing their shit.

'We're so proud of you, Matthew,' said Mum, planting a kiss on my cheek. 'We know you've got to get ready for work, but how about a bit of cake?'

They sat on the end of my bed, behind them a large black and white poster of the wrestler, Hulk Hogan. Together, under Hogan's watchful gaze, the three of us ate birthday cake for breakfast.

While I'd love to pretend my parents were just super buzzed about birthdays, there was another reason they were making such a fuss. Today marked six months since I'd started a new job with Southern United Community Care, or SUCC for short, a private company which offered in-home care to old people. I get that this might not seem like a big deal, but since finishing high school, I'd never stuck to anything for six months.

My friends went to university, and I tagged along, but where they found their feet, I lost my footing. Over two years, I started and stopped three – count 'em: one, two, three – university degrees: Journalism, Law and Education.

None were quite the right fit: I was too lazy to be a journalist, too impatient to be a lawyer and *way* too angry for teaching. With each fresh dropout, my parents would sit me down and deliver a different version of the same 'Where do you see yourself?' speech.

It didn't help that I'd recently been earning pocket money on the pro-wrestling circuit, a hobby my parents hated, though, ironically, it was their intervention that led me to the ring.

Growing up I'd had a quick temper and at school, teachers would pull my mother aside to say things like, 'Matthew is a handful', or 'He's hyperactive'. 'Hyperactive' was a word they loved to use.

'Yes, he's a real ... bundle of energy,' she would reply, nervously wondering if I was a dud.

At the suggestion of a counsellor, my parents enrolled me in every team sport imaginable: basketball, soccer, football, baseball. You name it, I failed at it.

It wasn't until I turned eighteen and discovered professional wrestling – where the outcome is predetermined and over the top anger is encouraged – that I found a way of channelling my energy.

One visit to a local gym and I was hooked. I loved the way wrestling blurred the line between real pain and staged drama. I trained and performed nonstop for four years wrestling under the name – wait for it – Tiny Tantrum. My whole schtick was that I was a giant toddler with a bad temper. I even wore a nappy. Bizarre, right?

Lately I'd returned to the circuit, getting paid a few hundred bucks to wrestle in small shows, mostly in RSL clubs and scout halls. Whenever I came home bruised, sore and rocking heavy eye make-up I'd catch a loaded look between my parents. *What do we do now?*

After a recent match ended in a busted eye socket (mine), and a broken arm (the other guy's), my parents managed to convince me it was time to hang up the leotard and 'get serious about growing up'.

In between degree-hopping and wrestling, I also tried acting (two months), working at a bar (three weeks, two days) and Uber driving (three trips). So yeah, the fact I had hung on at SUCC six months without getting bored, hurt, or fired, damn right that called for cake.

Like I said, the more you disappoint, the lower the bar.

'Mum, this is seriously good,' I said, shovelling the cake in. Dad grunted in agreement; he'd already hoovered his piece down and was making a start on Mum's.

'You're very welcome, and like I said, we're so, so proud of you, aren't we Peter!'

She nudged Dad to remind him he should chuck in his two cents. A bunch of crumbs had taken up residence in his thick mo'. They danced as he spoke.

'Yeah mate, happy birthday,' he said, offering his hand for me to shake. 'Glad to see you're getting yourself together. Honestly, I wouldn't have picked it.'

Dad's backhanded compliment was cut short by the all-too-familiar buzz of my phone alarm.

'Okay! Well, your father and I will get out of your hair,' said Mum. 'But I'll see you for lunch, and don't forget I'm bringing Nan in, too. My shout!'

Cake for breakfast and a free lunch, this birthday was shaping up nicely.

****

When I first started applying for real-world adult jobs, I gave myself little-to-no chance of being hired. My CV was incredibly lacklustre and only months later did I realise my name was misspelt.

No one was beating down the door to hire *Natthew*.

Out of the thirty plus roles I applied for Southern United Community Care was the first (and only) company to offer an interview, which is how I found myself in the office of Gavin Rogers, managing partner, SUCC.

We sat opposite each other while he clicked away at the computer. Each time Gavin leant forward to look at the screen, I spied the dent of his body moulded into the chair, like he'd been sitting there forever.

That was very much the vibe Gavin gave off, a resigned defeat that he would die right here in this suffocating room. He turned towards me, reading the job criteria out loud like a shopping list.

Did I want to make a real difference in the aged care sector?

Was I looking for a dynamic company with a vibrant work culture?

Could this be an opportunity for growth in a positive and supportive team environment?

My honest answers were no, no and probably not, but that didn't stop me laying it on thick. Gavin may have given up, but I needed this.

'Ever since I can remember it's been a dream to work in aged care services,' I began, cringing at how insincere the words sounded. Gavin was already frowning at me; things were going badly. I glanced down at my notes: *What was the job again?*

Client liaison officer: You will be the first point of contact for clients, families and carers.
Responsibilities: Matching appropriate carers with the most suitable clients. Coordinating rosters. Some weekend work.

'Not only am I passionate about coordinating rosters, but I am open to some weekend work!'

Gavin held up a hand to cut me off. 'Look, Matt, wait: is it Matt or Matthew?' he asked.

'Either is fine.' *Just not Natthew.*

'Right, Matt. No one is as passionate about coordinating rosters as you claim to be, okay?'

Good point.

'I know you don't have much experience.' He paused and held my CV up as proof, a single piece of paper pinched sadly between two fingers. 'But I'm going to give you a chance. Forget whatever you think I want to hear and just do a good job. SUCC is a great place to start, we've got a decent team, and there's plenty of opportunity for a young guy like you.'

Gavin handed me some paperwork and walked me to the door. 'Who knows, you might just end up enjoying yourself.'

That was six months ago and much to my surprise, he was on the money. The job itself was fine. As Gavin predicted it's hard to be passionate about organising rosters, but the rigid order of office life seemed to agree with me.

I liked getting the 8.07 train each morning. I liked buying a coffee from a man who remembered my name and I liked walking into work and sitting at my own desk with my own things. I even liked popping into the kitchen and chatting weekend plans with Jenny from accounts. Usually our plans were very different, but still, it felt *grown up* – which is exactly what my parents had wanted.

After so many false starts, the stability of nine-to-five couldn't have come at a better time. Did I want to eventually take over from Gavin and carve out my own depressing body mould in the hot seat? Not a chance.

But for now, being a client liaison officer suited me fine.

****

Monday mornings in the office were my favourite part of the week, much to the dismay of Jan and Helen, my two desk buddies.

'You've got to be the only person I know who likes Mondays,' said Jan, dousing her keyboard in Ajax, before passing the Spray 'n' Wipe to Helen. This was how they began each day, a ceremonial cleansing of the workspace.

'Monday, Tuesday, Friday, they're all the same when you've been here this long,' laughed Helen.

Jan and Helen were actually half the reason I enjoyed Mondays. After an entire weekend doing stupid shit with my dumb friends, it was refreshing to be around their wholesome mother energy.

At best guess, I put them both around sixty-five years old, though they refused to confirm exactly. 'Never ask a woman her age, Matthew,' Helen would say.

The same rule didn't apply in reverse. 'You're how old today?' asked Jan.

'Twenty-two,' I replied, tapping the '22 and READY

TO PARTY!' badge Helen had pinned to my shirt earlier. She'd also covered my desk in streamers and balloons.

'Oh my god, you're a child, you're a baby, you're an infant.' Jan shot a look at Helen, who joined in on the ribbing: 'Twenty-two! I have underpants older than you, Matthew.'

We all smiled. Since starting the job Jan and Helen had taken me under their wing, and the three of us had developed a strange yet easy rapport, two doting mother hens and their pseudo-son.

They mocked me for having no idea about the real world, or my place in it, and I gave it back to them for being, well, old. 'You still wear underpants? I thought you'd be in adult nappies by now!'

'Careful young man,' said Helen, popping a balloon with her finger. 'I'd hate to burst your bubble on your birthday!'

The other reason that I loved Mondays is because it was Ashley Sinclair's rostered day off. Ashley was second-in-charge but a first-class punish. From the minute I set foot in the office we didn't click.

Initially, I thought Ashley hated me because I could talk to people, whereas she seemed physically pained by social interaction. Greet her in the lift, and she'd sink into herself, plumbing the depths of her soul for a spare 'hello'.

But chatting came naturally to me and flanked by my two work mums, I became the charming young fool of the office.

Over afternoon tea, I'd share sordid tales from my weekend about late nights, dirty kebabs and one-night stands, and everyone would laugh along: 'Oh, to be young again!'

Then Ashley would walk past, scowling, and a hush would fall over the group. The second she was out of earshot, we'd pick up where we left off. 'Tell us again about the girl you snuck out the back door!'

It also didn't help that I was oblivious to the office hierarchy. I understood that Gavin was the boss but assumed the rest of us were on an equal playing field. This didn't sit well with Ashley, who used every opportunity to remind me she was 'Two IC', whatever that meant.

'Matthew, as you know, I'm Two IC.'

'I thought you were second-in-charge?'

'Yes, I am.'

'So, who is Two IC?'

'Me! It's the same thing!'

Whenever Ashley would call me out for a mistake, or comment on my occasional lateness, I couldn't help but bite back.

'You realise you took an hour and a half for lunch today?'

She always made sure to say these things loudly, so everyone heard.

'Yes, I know, I'm sorry, as Three IC I should set a better example.'

Naive and a smart ass, killer combo.

Looking back, she had every right to be wary of me. Ashley was in her mid-thirties, a smart career-driven woman working her way up the corporate ladder. I was a twenty-two-year-old know-it-all who loved wrestling and spent most Fridays yelling 'T-G-I-F!' to anyone who'd listen.

Obviously, I should've been more concerned about keeping Ashley onside, but at the time I simply didn't care. The middle-aged brigade loved me; I had safety in numbers. Everything was going to be just fine; I was certain.

So certain in fact, that when I received a meeting request from Human Resources – first thing on a Monday, the morning of my birthday – I hit accept and didn't think twice.

****

'Matthew, how do you think you're going?'

Let's pause for a moment right here. If you're ever asked this question at work, and it doesn't send shivers down your spine, then let me be the bearer of bad news: You're about to get fired.

'Really well actually, I'm enjoying the work, the team is great. I feel like I'm learning a lot.'

Bianca Stone let out a deep sigh. As the HR manager, this was undoubtedly the worst part of her job, and I wasn't making it any easier.

'I still have a way to go, but yeah, so far so good, I think? I'd love to talk next steps; I know I've only been here a little while, but.'

Much like Gavin had done six months prior, Bianca held up a hand to silence me.

'We see things differently.'

The words hung in the air, and I could tell Bianca was willing me to catch up; catch on. She was used to dealing with people who knew the dance: she summoned them, and they walked the plank. Brutal but professional. I did her no favours.

'Go on.' At this point, Bianca benched any effort to sugar-coat it and resorted to reading from a prepared statement.

'This letter confirms our discussion today that your employment with Southern United Community Care is terminated for cause, effective immediately.

'Your employment, as discussed during the termination meeting, is terminated as a result of a failure to onboard feedback from senior staff, as well as consistent breaches regarding company policy and our code of conduct.'

My head was spinning, but Bianca didn't let up, she went on and on. Who knew there were so many different versions of 'you're fired'.

'Cessation of employment ... discontinue your position ... conclude all roles and responsibilities.'

Finally, she stopped talking – sorry, *terminated her words* – and slid the letter across the desk.

I rewound the conversation in my head, snippets flashing across my brain. If I could just reach out and touch one it might make sense – *failure to onboard feedback from senior staff.*

'Ashley.'

To her credit, Bianca had done a bang-up job of keeping things professional so far. Her voice never wavered; she persevered despite my inability to follow. Top marks for termination.

But at the mention of Ashley, she dropped her guard for a split second, but long enough for me to notice.

'Matthew, this isn't about any one person.'

'Ashley got me fired?'

'As it states in the letter, your performance has been –' I didn't even let her finish.

'I'd like to speak with Gavin please.'

'I don't know if that's necessary,' Bianca replied. 'Why don't you take some time, pack your things and then we can go over.'

I butted in. 'No, I think it *is* necessary.'

Ashley had terminated new-and-improved adult Matthew – on his birthday! I deserved answers.

'Fine, if that's what you want. Gavin will be in shortly, until then please keep this confidential.'

Sure thing.

Back at my desk, Jan and Helen were already waiting.

'Ashley just got me fucking fired!'

They nodded in a way that was both sympathetic but unsurprised. While I failed to understand the gravity of a meeting with HR, clearly they had not. 'I'm so sorry, Matthew,' said Jan, gazing at the birthday streamers on my desk. 'Want us to help clean this stuff up?'

'No, it's okay, I'm waiting to see Gavin.' Jan and Helen exchanged a disapproving look, but I ignored it.

If you've ever worked in an office, you'll be fully aware that drama takes off like a house fire– time to throw gasoline on the gossip and watch it burn. I made my way around the cubicles, fanning the flames.

'Ashley got me fired.'

'Yeah, she basically got me terminated, I know, right?'

'Discontinued my employment!'

By the time I'd done a lap, word had spread, and I started to convince myself I could engineer a mutiny. Did they really want to terminate me, the lovable fool? The naive no-hoper who was just learning the ropes!?

I was honestly minutes away from standing on my chair and going full Jerry Maguire: *'Who's coming with me?'*

But then Gavin walked in, and I witnessed a hushed conversation between him and Bianca. He rolled his eyes so violently I feared they would pop out, then looked at me and jerked his head in the direction of his office.

****

'What don't you understand, mate?'

Gavin clicked away at the computer, half-distracted. Even the act of firing me didn't demand his full attention. This felt much like the first time I'd sat in this sad office, except sadder.

'Ah, well, I spoke with Bianca, and I'm just a little confused.'

He turned to face me. 'You're confused, are you? Let me make it clear for you.'

Having only experienced Bianca's softly-softly approach, Gavin's directness was very confronting. Finger-counting, he reeled off different reasons to fire me.

'You're underperforming month-on-month, your lunch breaks go for hours, you're too slow on the phones, you have a bad temper, and if it wasn't for Jan and Helen, I don't think you'd have a clue what you're doing.'

By the time he finished all that remained was his full hand in front of my face: *Pick any one of five reasons I should fire your dumb ass.*

He made a compelling case, and I knew it was over, so I figured I might as well ask the question on everyone's lips: 'And Ashley?'

Gavin leaned across the desk, conspiratorially. 'You want to know what I think of Ashley?'

He kicked back in his chair, slotting deep into the well-worked groove.

'I think ... she makes my life easier, and you make her life harder, so that's all I need to know.'

And with that, my termination was complete. Just as he did six months earlier, Gavin ushered me to the door, and we lingered awkwardly both unsure of the post-firing etiquette. A hug is off the cards and shaking hands feels too congratulatory. Instead, we just nodded at each other.

'What's with that?' Gavin asked, tapping my chest.

I'd forgotten the badge was still pinned to my shirt. 'Oh, it's my birthday.'

'Ah, of course. Happy birthday then.'

No happy returns.

* * * * * * *

Every wrestler needs a memorable finisher, a signature move that fans come to expect each match. All the greats had killer calling cards: Hulk Hogan's leg drop, Shawn Michaels' sweet chin music and my all-time favourite, Steven Austin's Stone-Cold Stunner.

The Stunner was a thing of beauty: simple, yet spectacular.

First, he would fold his opponent in half with a high kick to the guts. Once their head was in position, he would wrap an arm around their neck and hurl them to the mat.

Usually, they'd hit the deck with an extremely satisfying *pop!* and then Austin would celebrate by cracking an ice-cold beer and tipping it over their motionless body. Masterful.

When I first started wrestling, I worried that my persona, Tiny Tantrum, didn't lend itself to any Stunner-style finishers. I tried a few different moves, but nothing really worked, until one day the perfect finisher found me in aisle three of the local grocery store.

Mum and I were grabbing something for dinner when we stumbled on a classic supermarket blow up: a red-faced toddler versus a father on the verge of a mental breakdown. From what I could gather, the dad had banned all the fun food from the weekly shop and was now copping an absolute pounding for it.

As the child rained his fists down upon his maker's chest, I was captivated by the vicious choreography.

'Don't stare, Matthew,' said Mum, but how could I not?

At that moment, the Fists of Fury were born, and from then on, whenever I had an opponent dazed in the ring, I would finish them with a series of blows to the chest.

Sadly, the Fists had been packed away since I stopped wrestling. No need for a silly finisher because I was a grown-up adult with a 'Real Job'. Except I wasn't any more. Now I was an ex-employee headed home at 11 am on a Monday after being fired on my birthday.

Ding. The elevator opened, and a smartly dressed woman looked up from her phone. 'Going up?'

'No,' I told her. 'Going down.'

I bashed the down button in that futile-but-frustrated way – you know it does nothing and yet you do it anyway. I didn't need to turn around to register the full attention of the office. I could sense their eyes on my back, a sea of faces watching but pretending not to. *Where is this elevator?*

Eventually, another *ding* and the doors wheezed open. There was no one in the lift, but it felt crowded with people: my disappointed parents, Bianca, Gavin, Jan, Helen, Ashley the Two I-C, all suffocating the space, yelling over the top of each other.

With each passing floor, their rumble grew louder, until the lift melted away and I was back in the ring. Tiny Tantrum once more, spurred on by the deafening chant of an impatient crowd.

'FISTS OF FURY, FISTS OF FURY!'

In a split second, I gave the people what they wanted, surrendered control, pounding the doors with everything I had, and everything I had lost.

'FISTS OF FURY!'

The lift jerked and swayed before releasing a howling mechanical grumble. This can't be good. For a few seconds, the walls shuddered, whined, and then the lift came to a ball-tingling stop: no movement, no noise, no anything.

In a situation like this, you immediately start weighing up your options.

Option one: The quick fix.

You pray that whatever you try first works out, otherwise your minor mistake turns into a major shit show. I pushed the ground floor button: *please work, please work*. No dice.

Option two: The waiting game.

Decide the best course of action is to do nothing. Maybe the lift just needs a few minutes to cool off, and it'll go back to regular working order. Time ticked away, but the lift didn't move.

Option three: The obvious one.

Do what you're supposed to. Taunting me at the bottom of the control panel was a red emergency button. If I pressed it, a call would connect me to the emergency repair team.

The answer is always option three, even when you don't want it to be.

'Hello, Edgecliff Urgent Lift Repairs.'

'Hi, I'm stuck in a lift.'

'Okay, can you confirm your location?'

After a bit of back and forth, the floating elevator voice told me to sit tight and relax.

'Don't worry, mate. We'll send someone out to get you, it should be half an hour tops. And don't go anywhere, HA-HA!'

Adding to my woes was the fact I couldn't even Google: *can you suffocate in an elevator?* because my reception had dropped out. Not that I needed to worry about being left to die. I'd busted the only elevator in the building, so the breakdown quickly became a logistical talking point.

'Looks like the lift is broken.'

'Yeah, I think you're right.'

'Reckon anyone's in there?'

I could hear echoed voices discussing my predicament. They came from above and below me, meaning I was stuck between two floors.

'Yes, hello, I'm here!' I shouted back to them.

'Shit, there is someone down there. Are you okay?'

Well, they asked: 'Umm, not really, I just got fired.'

It's an awkward bit of information to volunteer so readily to people, especially strangers, *especially* when you're trapped in an elevator shame prison. *Why did I say that?*

Even from down in the lift, I felt this comment land with a thud, followed by panicked whispers.

'I think he said he just got fired!'

'Is that what you heard?'

'Oh god, this is so awkward, the poor guy!'

The acoustics of the elevator shaft meant their every word reverberated loudly in the lift.

'I can hear you, you know!'

'Sorry. Where did you work, did you want us to go grab someone?'

Great question: who do you lean on in this very unusual crisis? Gavin had just fired me, and I didn't want Jan and Helen to see me, or at least *hear* me, like this.

'No, it's okay,' I shouted back. 'I'll just chill here. The repair guys shouldn't be too long.'

* * * * * * *

How many urgent lift repairs are happening in the city at the same time? This is the question I asked myself as another gruelling hour dragged past. So much for 'half an hour tops'.

As if it wasn't bad enough being trapped inside an elevator, I was now dealing with two further problems. One of the whisperers had alerted Gavin, who was now keeping a lift-side vigil.

'Hang in there, mate, we're all here for you!' he yelled, no doubt worried I might die and the last thing that ever happened to me was getting sacked by him.

'We're going to pull through this together!'

'Just like when you fired me?' Silence.

The other issue was that a calendar alert had just flashed up on my phone: *1.00 pm: B'DAY LUNCH WITH MUM AND NAN :-)*

In all the drama of the birthday termination, I hadn't had a chance to text Mum and bin lunch and with no reception I couldn't reach her. She prides herself on being punctual, so there was no doubt in my mind she would be currently pacing the lobby wondering why I was late.

This thought was overrun by the shrill of heavy machinery.

'Matty? Mate are you there?' asked Gavin, his voice meek with guilt.

'Yes Gavin, where else would I be?'

'Good one. Okay, well the technicians are here, so I'm going to hand over to them, and we're gonna get you out of there buddy!'

Considering how ridiculous the whole episode had been, the path to freedom felt borderline anticlimactic. Using the jaws of life, two technicians prised the doors open and winched me to safety.

Back on solid ground, it was oddly quiet. I don't know what I expected, well-wishers perhaps?

Everyone was gone; even Gavin had made himself scarce. Just me and my rescuers.

'Thanks, guys, appreciate the effort.'

'No worries', said the shorter man whose voice I recognised from the control box. 'Is it your birthday?' asked his colleague, pointing at my badge.

'Yeah, it is actually.'

The two men laughed, and the shorter man shook his head in disbelief.

'How's that for birthday luck! Hopefully, your day gets better from here, mate.'

The only way is up, I thought, taking the stairs to the ground floor.

* * * * * * *

As is often the case with Mum, I heard her before I saw her.

'He's only been there six months,' she explained, her familiar voice bouncing across the lobby.

The staircase spat me out near the emergency exit, on the far side of the ground floor. Lunchtime meant it was heaving with action, but Mum had a way of cutting through.

'His current role is case liaison officer … or is it client liaison officer … something to do with liaising, but I think he'll move through the ranks quickly, he seems so *switched on*.'

Eventually, the crowd thinned out and Mum and Nan came into view, the pair of them waiting together, all dressed up. A wrapped gift sat on Nan's lap while Mum wrestled with a birthday balloon that seemed desperate to escape.

From where I was standing, I could see them, but they couldn't see me.

'Anyway, you can ask Matthew all about it over lunch,' said Mum, patting Nan on the leg.

She sounded proud and excited, which broke me a little. For the first time that day I stopped feeling sorry for myself and started feeling sorry for her. I knew that soon enough I'd have to tell my parents what had gone down. Explain the whole Ashley and Gavin situation, and the elevator, and the Fists of Fury.

No doubt all of the above would prompt a fresh wave of disappointment; another *'where do you see yourself?'* speech. But for now, or at least the rest of the afternoon, I could make the right decision in a day full of wrong calls. I could pretend to be Mum's still-employed son a little longer.

'Mum! Nan! So sorry to keep you waiting,' I said, stepping into frame and giving them both a hug. 'Been a busy day, had a couple of key clients I needed to liaise with.'

'Key clients!' repeated Mum, turning to Nan and grinning.

'Well, that's totally fine sweetheart. Are you sure you can still do lunch?'

'I can do you one better,' I said, opening the lobby door and ushering them both into the afternoon sun. 'The boss gave me the rest of the day off!'

THE F*** UP HALL OF FAME

Crash Into (and All Over) Me

> **Name**: Stefan Wohl   **Rating**: 9/10
>
> **Fuck-up**: Illegally dumping 360 kilos of human sewage out the back of a tour bus and into the Chicago River, unaware it was actually landing on a boat full of sightseers passing below.

Every so often a set of circumstances collide so spectacularly that a fuck-up seems to be written in the stars, an act of fate preordained by a higher power. That's the only way you can explain what went down in the city of Chicago on 8 August 2004.

Emo rock gods the Dave Matthews Band were midway through a sold-out summer tour of the United States. So far the band had blown away audiences in Florida, Texas, North Carolina and Georgia, but their most explosive performance was yet to come.

With two shows booked at the Alpine Valley Music Theatre in Wisconsin, the band had set up camp in Chicago. This is typical for big acts: Chicago is a major city and Wisconsin is only a little under two hours away by bus.

On the morning of 8 August, the band was prepping for their second show at Alpine Valley.

In proof that rock-and-roll excess was still well and truly alive in the mid-noughties, each member of the Dave Matthews Band had their own tour bus.

Unnecessary? Yes. Perfect for this story? Absolutely.

Around midday, Stefan Wohl, the driver assigned to violinist Boyd Tinsley's tour bus, was summoned to a Michigan Avenue hotel to pick Boyd up so he wouldn't be late for rehearsals.

The route Stefan chose that day sent him downtown and across the Kinzie Street Bridge, which runs above the Chicago River. Like most significant bridges in Chicago, the Kinzie Street Bridge features open metal grating, which allows rain to pass through easily.

Having been on the road for nearly two months, it was no surprise that the tour bus's septic tank was near overflowing. Eight weeks' worth of human waste transported on eighteen wheels.

Crossing east over the bridge at 1.18 pm, Stefan must've clocked that the shitter was full and decided there was no better place than the Chicago River to empty the septic tank. Hitting a toggle behind the driver's seat, he released the waste.

Now the Chicago River is home to many tourist attractions but none more popular than the Chicago River Architecture

Boat Tour. Voted number one on TripAdvisor, the boat ride promises guests an afternoon they'll never forget. Boy, how right they were.

At the exact moment Stefan dropped *360 kilos of human sewage* out of the tour bus, 109 unlucky tourists were passing under the Kinzie Street Bridge.

Nearly everyone on board the boat, *The Little Lady*, was drenched in the excrement. As a torrent of turd rained down upon them, they must've thought 'this is an afternoon we will truly never ever forget'.

Oblivious to the literal shitstorm he had just created, Stefan drove away but a passenger, onboard *Little Lady* managed to jot down the bus licence plate. It wasn't long before the Chicago PD tracked down both Stefan and the Dave Matthews Band.

Faecal fuck-ups have a funny way of catching up with you.

In March 2005 Stefan pleaded guilty to misdemeanour charges of reckless conduct and water pollution. He was fined US$10,000, sentenced to 18 months' probation and given 150 hours of community service. The Dave Matthews Band eventually agreed to pay US$200,000 to settle a lawsuit with the city of Chicago.

Following the trial, Chicago mayor Richard M. Daley reminded everyone that 'the action of illegally dumping in the Chicago River is absolutely unacceptable', before conceding that the Dave Matthews Band are 'a very good band'.

TODAY I F****D UP

Perhaps the most heartbreaking part of this story is that many of the tourists on board had tickets to see the Dave Matthews Band that same evening.

Adding a whole new meaning to the term *shit hit the fan*.

Do You See What I See?

Oliver's story

I'm not ashamed to admit that when I decided to become a doctor the part I was most excited about, besides saving lives of course, was my aeroplane moment.

You know the one I mean: you see it in movies and TV shows all the time. A passenger falls ill and someone yells out: *Is there a doctor on board?*

I would calmly raise my hand, rip my shirt open Superman-style to reveal a stethoscope: *Yes, it is I: I am a doctor.*

But once I started actually studying medicine, the most exciting part, besides learning how to save lives of course, was my newfound ability to sleep whenever or wherever I got the chance.

So demanding is the coursework, so intense are the expectations, that sleep is constantly in short supply. If you're able to carve out a spare five minutes in between memorising every bone in the body (there are *so many*), you take it.

It's a skill that never goes away either, even once you finish training. These days I work in hospitals surrounded by colleagues who can drift off the second they're not required. Yes, as well as being adept at diagnosing, prescribing, slicing and dicing, doctors are unrivalled when it comes to impromptu sleeping.

Which presents a problem with my 'Is there a doctor on board?' aeroplane fantasy, because plane naps are among the most satisfying of naps. So, while a doctor may indeed be on board, it is highly likely they will be dozing come the hour of need.

It's just what we're good at.

* * * * * * *

Years earlier

'Oliver, wake up!'

Alex shook me violently and leant across my lap.

'I *knew* you'd fall asleep. I *knew* I should've taken the window seat,' she complained, craning her neck to peer out my window.

We were on a tiny plane, flying to a tiny island, and by the looks of it, minutes away from landing on a very tiny airstrip.

'That can't be the runway, Alex,' I said, rubbing my eyes. 'It's about ten metres long.'

'Twenty-five metres actually,' she corrected, consulting her Cook Islands guidebook. This was in 2011 when guidebooks, not smartphones, were still the most reliable source of information.

'First constructed in the 1970s, Atiu Airport was built on the plateau close to the villages. In 1982 it was discovered that the runway was too short and could not be extended.'

'Discovered' sounded like a convenient way of glossing over a plane crash.

'And how was it discovered exactly?' I asked, picturing an overshot landing and fiery wreckage.

Alex ignored me and continued reading: 'In 1984 the building of the airport near the beach was undertaken. Atiu Island was originally known as Enuamanu, or Island of Birds, and has a population of 410 people.'

By the looks of it, all 410 locals were waiting for us as our plane hurtled towards the runway. I prayed we would discover this runway was long enough.

'Ladies and gentlemen, welcome to Atiu Island,' buzzed the overhead announcement. 'Local time is ten o'clock, but in this little slice of paradise, don't be surprised if you forget time exists at all!'

Alex packed her guidebook away and nodded. 'Slice of paradise, Oliver,' she said, squeezing my hand. 'After the last month, even a slice will do. Now get me a cocktail!'

We were in the last few weeks of a gruelling three-month overseas placement which was required as part of the final year of our medical degree.

Alex and I met on the first day of university when she picked out the exact building I was searching for before I'd even had a chance to ask for help.

'Health science is that way,' she said, pointing to a grand sandstone building in the distance. She spoke without looking up, her head buried in a university textbook.

That moment set the tone for the rest of our friendship; Alex called the shots while I followed her lead. When the time came for our three-month overseas study placement, we stuck to this same pattern.

'I have family in the Solomon Islands,' explained Alex. 'We can stay with them while we complete the placement and on the weekends they can show us the *real* Solomon Islands.'

As a cautious traveller who mostly enjoys the hotel portion of holidays, I knew I'd prefer the *sanitised* Solomon Islands: crystal blue water and cocktails, like in the brochures.

But Alex's enthusiasm was infectious, and so the real Solomon Islands awaited us. Unfortunately, a month before we left, a *real* political coup took place, and it was agreed the Cook Islands might be a safer alternative. So for the past two months we had been living and studying on Rarotonga, the largest of the Cook Islands.

Balancing island life with study might sound idyllic but the reality was a different story: fewer hammocks, far more headaches. If we weren't spending twelve hours a day at the local clinic, we were trying, and failing, to keep up with our prescribed course reading.

After eight weeks the placement had taken its toll and lately we'd both been desperate for a weekend off. According to Alex's trusty guidebook, Atiu was the perfect place to unwind, a slice of paradise that promised a little peace and quiet.

'TAXI, TAXI, TAXI' came the chorus of offers the minute we stepped out of the airport and into the sunlight. Ah yes, peace and quiet. Through the throng of locals, I spotted a man holding a handwritten sign that read MR ALEX.

'After you, sir,' I said to Alex, gesturing to the sign. Never one to leave anything to chance Alex had pre-booked our driver, who was waving at us from across the carpark.

'Welcome to Atiu, friends,' he beamed, ushering us into his van. 'I am Rua!'

Alex rode up front and began grilling Rua on all things Atiu, her dog-eared guidebook a giveaway of the too-keen tourist.

I tried to contribute to the conversation, though the bumpy ride made it tough to stay awake. The flight from Rarotonga was only forty-five minutes, but despite my plane nap fatigue had settled in and I was desperate for a shower, a meal, a nap, and a beer, in that exact order.

At some point, I must've drifted off but awoke with a start when I felt Rua kill the engine. Peeling my face off the window, I looked outside, expecting to see a hotel, some friendly locals, maybe even a pool bar. Instead, we had stopped near the water's edge.

'Are you excited to fish?' asked Rua, smiling at me through the rear-view mirror.

Wait, what?

Clocking my confusion, Rua turned around and pointed to a bucket next to me: three rusty fishing reels and a packet of fresh bait. 'I take you fishing,' he said, hopping out of the car.

'Atiu is home to some of the best spots in the islands.'

I tapped Alex on the shoulder before she could join Rua for the fishing expedition.

'What happened to "now get me a cocktail"?' I asked, eyeing the reels in horror.

'Rua offered to take us when you fell asleep,' she replied, putting both hands up in mock surrender. 'You know I can't say no to people!'

'And *you* know I'm not outdoorsy!'

Alex rolled her eyes. My preference for indoor activities had been a bone of contention since we'd arrived on placement. She wanted to hike, I wanted to play cards; she wanted to see the sunrise, I wanted a tequila sunrise.

Outside the van we watched Rua push a small dinghy off the bank and into the water.

'Don't be so precious,' said Alex. 'Anyway, I've organised a non-fishing activity later this afternoon.'

'Something cruisy like abseiling I hope?'

'Funny,' said Alex, without actually laughing. 'No, but it involves drinking so we'll both enjoy it.'

Comforted by the promise of future cocktails, I slid the van door open to find Rua smiling his delightful smile. 'The boat is ready; you are excited?'

I'd never been less excited to do anything in my life.

'Can't wait, Rua!'

* * * * * * *

Whenever I'm doing something I don't enjoy, like floating on a rickety boat in the middle of the South Pacific Ocean,

I tend to talk about things I do enjoy as a way of regaining control.

'Rua, have you had much experience with ciguatera poisoning?' I asked, thinking fondly back to first-year medicine. The study of infectious diseases formed part of our early coursework, and I had thrived while learning about the different complex infections that can attack the body.

'I know it,' said Rua, reeling in another fish from the sea. He seemed to have them on a string.

The three of us watched it flip-flop hopelessly on the deck.

'It is the most common seafood illness reported in travellers to the Cook Islands,' I continued. 'Caused by consuming fish contaminated with ciguatoxins which are produced by dinoflagellates – small marine organisms living on or near coral reefs – belonging to the species *Gambierdiscus toxicus*.'

Alex gazed at me, slack-jawed. 'Can you kill it with the ciguatera chat, Oliver? You're scaring the fish.'

'It's us who should be scared,' I replied.

'The disease has a range of symptoms, anything from mild abdominal pain, nausea and vomiting, to more serious symptoms like temperature reversal, blurred vision and even temporary blindness.'

Rua hauled in another colourful fish from the ocean, but he was no longer smiling. I appeared to have sucked all the fun from our fishing trip.

'Oliver!' scolded Alex in a way that I understood to mean, *Oliver! Fix this mess.*

'Usually, it's mild,' I offered, hoping this might soften the blow. 'But occasionally it can kill people or paralyse them.'

Following my 'Ciguatera can kill' speech, we floated quietly; the silence interrupted only by Alex passive aggressively reeling her fishing line in while glaring at me. Eventually, Rua spoke up, bringing an end to the oppressive stillness.

'Don't worry, Mr Oliver,' he said, the grin returning to his face. 'On Rarotonga plenty of fish poisoning but here on Atiu, no cases for fifteen years, maybe more. I'll prove it!' And with that Rua kickstarted the motor and we headed for the shore.

Back on dry land, the collective mood seemed to lift, Alex forgave me for lecturing Rua about infectious diseases, and I made it up to him by helping prepare lunch on the beach. Our catch of the day was on the menu, and as Rua passed me a piece of charred parrotfish, I could see Alex trying not to laugh. 'Can you taste the ciguatera?' she joked.

'Delicious, no?' asked Rua, picking at his plate. It was actually and, teamed with a few ice-cold beers, my concerns about foodborne illnesses quickly washed away.

After lunch, Rua stood up, turning to survey the paradise that stretched out in front of us. So perfect was the view it reminded me of a desktop screensaver: palm trees gently swaying in the breeze, blue sky meeting blue water.

'Magical,' said Alex, and it was hard to disagree.

'So, Mr Oliver,' said Rua, spinning to face me. 'You fish, you eat, and now . . . you *tumunu*?'

* * * * * * *

'TU-MU-NU,' announced Alex, flicking through her guidebook until she found the right page.

'A traditional Atiu bush bar that has been around for over 200 years.'

She read aloud while we traipsed through the jungle, as ahead of us Rua used a machete to fend off the thick forest growth: 'Set in the jungle, the *tumunu* is a meeting place for expressing ideas, singing songs and solving problems, all washed down with bush beer brewed in a *tumunu* barrel carved from the base of a coconut tree.'

This was the surprise Alex had planned for our afternoon, and I had to admit it sounded like the perfect activity. Bush beer in a jungle bar: the best of both worlds.

After a quick pit stop at our accommodation, we were on the way to a nearby locals-only *tumunu* organised by Rua.

He explained that in the last few years, many of the *tumunu*s had transformed into popular tourist destinations, overrun by travellers who only wanted to 'pose for a picture and be on their way'. I knew the type, Rarotonga was crawling with them: American families in matching sandals; sunburnt Brits who marvelled at the weather even as it pinkened their skin.

I didn't mind them so much, but Alex took personal offence at their money pouches, cargo shorts and desire to capture every part of their holiday on camera.

'But stick with me,' said Rua, pausing in front of two towering palm fronds.

'And I will show you the true *tumunu*.'

He parted the palms to reveal a clearing under a woven canopy of trees. In the distance, six men sitting on tree trunks cheered at the sight of Rua. He ran ahead, and Alex fell into step alongside me. 'Beats the university bar back home.'

She wasn't wrong.

Walled in by towering trees on three sides, the *tumunu* took the form of a hut, with a thatched roof and makeshift bar. Above us the canopy was busy with birds, and their songs filled the air. Every so often they would dip and soar, swapping one tree for another. Sunlight filtered through the forest, throwing shadows across the clearing and giving the *tumunu* an almost magical glow.

I hate to use the word 'enchanting', but that's how it felt.

Rua made all the necessary introductions, the group eyeing us with a combination of curiosity and caution. Eventually, we took our seats in the circle and one of the locals walked us through the ceremony.

The way it worked was like this: a cup was filled with bush beer from the barrel, and a man sitting in the middle passed it around. When it was your turn, you had to finish the cup before handing it back.

As guests, Alex and I drank first, grimacing at the unfamiliar taste. Rua explained that the *tumunu* mix was made of oranges, malt, yeast and sugar.

'Island home-brew,' he said, slurping it down.

Years ago, I had attempted my own home-brew in a bathtub; the resulting liquor had smelt *and* tasted like feet. The bush beer was an improvement on my efforts and far more potent.

'Wow, that's really something,' coughed Alex, handing me the cup and exhaling deeply.

I could tell she was starting to feel it; I wasn't far behind. The *tumunu* didn't allow room for pacing oneself.

First, you could never control how much was in the cup, but you also couldn't pass it on until you'd drained every last drop. Second, you didn't want to sip too slowly because everyone was watching and waiting for their turn, so the pressure was on. The result? A bush beer buzz that turned strangers into best friends within the hour.

'So then Oliver says, "Hey Rua, you ever heard of ciguaterrrrrra?"' slurred Alex, joking at my expense. The men exploded with laughter, and I joined in, the home-brew making everything seem funnier, lighter.

With each lap of the circle, we became progressively looser and more relaxed. But then the daylight started to fade, and Rua stood up, telling us it was time to go.

'I must lead you back to your villa,' he said softly.

Alex and I looked at each other, one of those moments in a friendship when you know you're thinking the same thing. Here we were in the middle of the jungle, drinking island home-brew and trading life stories with men we'd never meet otherwise. The kind of experience you want to stretch out, not cut short.

'Rua, thank you so much for looking after us,' started Alex. 'But we're having such a great time, do you mind if we stay?'

The cheers of our new friends drowned out the tail end of her question; they enjoyed the company. Rua shifted uncomfortably on the spot.

'Do you remember the way?' he asked, pointing vaguely at the direction we'd come in.

'Definitely,' Alex and I said in unison, though I was sure neither of us did.

'Okay, well, I will see you tomorrow morning,' replied Rua, a hand on each of our shoulders.

'Don't forget, we have the Anatakitaki Cave tour, bright and early!'

Bright and early: two words you never want to hear when you're in the middle of a boozy bush beer session.

'Sounds good,' lied Alex, who was responsible for booking our crack-of-dawn cave tour. 'We'll be ready to go, first thing!'

Rua bade farewell to the rest of the bar and disappeared into the dusk, leaving Alex and me behind with our *tumunu* crew.

'Another cup?' asked the man in the middle, filling the coconut shell with home-brew and holding it out toward me.

Be rude not to.

* * * * * * *

All I could think as Alex and I drunkenly stumbled through the forest was: *why are forests so lovely in the daytime, and so terrifying at night?*

The dark had turned everything ominous, trees appearing as silent spooky strangers while we battled our way around and around in circles.

'You don't have your phone on you, do you?' asked Alex. Negative. We'd both left them charging at the villa, unaware we would be out so long.

'No, I don't. Wait, your guidebook doesn't come with a built-in flashlight?'

Even in the dark, I registered Alex's dirty look. Neither of us wanted to say it, but we were starting to panic.

As you may have caught on, we had overindulged at the *tumunu* after Rua left. One cup became two, became three, became four. Late in the drinking session, the men brewed up a fresh batch, promising us it would be even stronger than the last.

'Special,' whispered the man in the middle of the circle when handing me the cup.

By the time I was chain-smoking cigarettes and making up lyrics to local island hymns, I was feeling *special* indeed, and Alex was no better off. She had found herself in an impassioned conversation with one of the locals, Tupou, about the drought that was currently causing issues on Atiu. At one point, I was pretty sure she was sobbing.

Anyway, the rollicking *tumunu* party came to an abrupt end when our friends announced it was home time. After very brief goodbyes they hopped on motorbikes and took off, leaving Alex and me alone in the jungle. Drunk, dark and incredibly disorientated.

'Was it left here?' said Alex, pointing into an indiscriminate pitch-black vortex.

'I have no idea.'

'Goddamn it, Oliver,' she spat. 'Weren't you watching when Rua led the way?'

'No,' I hit back. 'I was listening to your oral history of *tumunu*s.'

My head was spinning, and I was sweating from every pore. Now wasn't the time to be fighting.

'Okay look, what about if we –' my attempted problem solving was interrupted by a single headlight and the purr of a motor.

Tupou on a motorbike.

'Are you lost?' asked the outline of Tupou. We explained to Tupou that yes, we were so very lost and so very drunk. He nodded a lot and swayed a little, which convinced me that he, too, was hammered.

'Wait here, five minutes,' he ordered, revving the bike back into gear and heading off.

Twenty minutes later, Tupou returned, this time driving a flatbed pickup truck. 'Hop in.'

'Hold up,' I said to Alex, who was already climbing aboard the tray. Not only was Tupou drunk, but he'd somehow traded up, motorbike for a truck. 'Where did he get this truck?'

'Does it matter?' said Alex.

Wanting to clear up any confusion, Tupou leaned out the window. 'I stole it.'

Great news, well, all aboard then!

'Do you have a better way of getting home?' asked Alex, noticing my hesitation. I did not but surely 'stolen truck with drunk driver' wasn't our only option?

Apparently it was and, as you can imagine, the ride home was absolutely white-knuckle terrifying. To this day, I can't really bring myself to dwell on it. Every bump in the road felt like our final moment on earth, and it was no small miracle that we arrived at the villa alive.

'This is us!' I yelled to Tupou, who brought the truck to a halt.

Safely on the ground, we were giddy with the adrenaline rush that comes from surviving a near-death experience. 'So that's the *real* Cook Islands then,' laughed Alex, fumbling in her handbag for our room key.

Behind me, the truck's engine came to life, and I turned to see Tupou with his head hanging out the driver side window, eyes glazed over.

'Do you see what I seeeee?' he yelled, driving off into the night.

No, I didn't, but I soon would.

* * * * * * *

Do you see what I see?

Back inside the villa, Alex peeled off to have a shower while I collapsed onto my bed, beaten by the bush beer.

Ironically, after all my boasts of 'whenever, wherever', sleep proved hard to come by. The room spun like a roulette wheel and I was too distracted by a rustling noise above my head.

Switching my bedside lamp on, I noticed several large cockroaches crawling out from underneath a tribal style cloth tapestry that hung above the bed. They were scattering in all directions, giant cockroaches, their movable antennae scanning every which way.

'ALEX, COME QUICK, COCKROACHES!' I yelled, frozen but mesmerised by their movement.

'I CAN'T HEAR YOU,' she yelled back. 'I'M IN THE SHOWER!'

I stopped for a second; something seemed off. No water was running, no steam escaping from under the door.

Keeping half my attention on the cockroach infestation, I backed slowly towards the bathroom, and gently pushed the door open using my foot. There stood a fully clothed Alex, mimicking all the actions of someone having a shower – soaping, shampooing, cleansing – but the water was off.

'Alex, what the hell are you doing?'

'OLIVER! Get out of here!'

I reached behind and turned on the tap, the splash of real water returning Alex to reality.

'Holy shit,' she said, looking down at her shampoo-sodden clothes. I handed Alex a towel, feeling drunker than I had in many years.

'You're a weirdo, now please come and help me with these roaches.'

Back in the bedroom, the roaches had multiplied ten, twenty times the amount I had seen before, and they seemed to be working in teams.

'You take the left side of the room, I'll take the right, and we'll meet in the middle,' I ordered, picking up two odd shoes and clobbering away.

Alex stayed perfectly still, seemingly undeterred by the insect onslaught.

'Oliver, what the hell are you doing?'

And that was when it dawned on us, the reason why we were standing there in our villa, me with my two odd shoes, Alex covered in shampoo but fully dressed. The 'special' batch of homebrew after Rua left, Tupou's final words: *Do you see what I see?*

'Holy shit,' said Alex, the wall behind her a moving canvas of cockroaches.

'We're tripping.'

Acknowledging it seemed to make things worse, and we both started hallucinating like crazy.

Everywhere I looked, roaches reigned supreme, and I was obsessed with trying to kill them.

'We have to finish them before they finish us,' I declared, jumping on the bed and hammering away at a blank wall.

I have no idea how long the killing spree lasted, only that I stopped when I heard Alex vomiting in the background.

'Oliver,' her voice barely audible from the bathroom.

'I think because of the drought on the island –' A long pause, intercut with her retching. '– I think, maybe, I am going to have to drink my own vomit.'

Despite my singular focus on roach-aggedon, a small, lucid, part of me knew this to be a terrible idea.

'Alex, you don't have to do that, you *mustn't* do that!'

'It's too late,' came the reply followed by another loud heave.

I rushed across the room and managed to stop Alex just before she consumed her own vomit, a real highpoint in our friendship.

Sitting on the bathroom floor, we stared at one another in disbelief. Neither of us had ever taken hallucinogens, but we had enough medical expertise to know that the only option was to ride it out.

'It's going to be fine. Everything will be fine.' I checked my watch; nearly one o'clock in the morning; hours had gone missing.

'Do my lips look big to you?' Alex asked, standing up to check her reflection in the bathroom mirror. I pulled myself up and stood behind her.

'No, they don't,' I said, though I couldn't really tell.

'Are you sure? They feel itchy!'

'It's just part of the trip; you feel sensations that aren't real.'

Alex nodded and yawned, which made me yawn also; finally, sleep had come to collect us.

'I'm going to have a shower now,' said Alex, pausing to consider her matted clothes.

'An *actual* shower.'

We said goodnight and I screwed my eyes shut as I stumbled into bed, desperate to avoid another cockroach attack.

Lying in the dark, I tried to ignore the trip, take deep breaths and just focus on what I knew to be true. Yes, Alex had switched the bathroom light on. Yes, Alex had started the shower.

Yes, Alex was *screaming for her life*. 'IT BURNS, IT BURNS!'

I bolted into the bathroom to find Alex shivering and the shower running stone cold.

'You're still tripping, Alex, the water is freezing,' I said, carrying her out of the bathroom and placing her on the bed. I wrapped her up in a towel, turned the shower off and came back to the room.

'Oliver, my skin is on fire, please, it's not the trip, get some ice or something!' begged Alex.

The fridge in our room was the size of a letterbox, so I held out little hope, but amazingly there was a small ice tray up top. Collecting a few cubes in a tea towel, I walked back to Alex.

'Where does it sting?'

'Everywhere,' she replied, grabbing the ice out of my hands.

And then: a second scream, worse than the first.

As Alex woke up the entire island of Atiu with her howls, something inside me shattered. The trip lifted, and the truth presented itself: *a diagnosis from the depths of my soul.*

Temperature reversal: When cold temperatures present as hot, resulting in increased hypersensitivity. So touching ice feels like handling fire.

Medically known as 'cold allodynia', a hallmark symptom of ciguatera.

****

Years later

It's only recently, with time, that I can look back on our weekend in Atiu and properly appreciate the irony. Two medical students catch the very disease they're wary of, and then fail to notice the symptoms because they're too busy tripping balls. What an episode that was.

To sum it up, as promised, Rua turned up bright and early the next day only to discover Alex and me at death's door. Naturally, because we had eaten the same fish, I also had ciguatera poisoning. Rua was fine.

The room had been turned upside down thanks mostly to my imaginative extermination. Turns out I'd even hallucinated the hanging tapestry; the wall was blank. I did feel a brief sense of justice after spying a single deceased cockroach near my bed.

Alex and I didn't move for nearly three days as ciguatera took control of our bodies. Gastric upsets, numbness and tingling in our hands and feet, and a terrible itch. Woefully unpleasant.

My symptoms only lasted a few weeks, but Alex's persisted for months, especially the cold sensitivity. It would be excruciating for her if she was outside and it rained, or if someone handed her a drink with ice in it.

Thankfully, the side effects eventually subsided and everything returned to normal. I'm still funny about eating seafood, though Alex is not. Recently we caught up for dinner, and she ordered the barramundi, which I found amusing.

'What?' she asked, as the waiter laid the fish out in front of her. I smiled back and sipped my beer, bottled, not bush.

'Tell me, can you taste the ciguatera?'

THE F*** UP HALL OF FAME

Death by Delayed Bullet

Name: Henry Ziegland **Rating**: 10/10

Fuck-up: Being struck and killed by the same bullet twenty years after it was first fired.

Growing up in Honey Grove, Texas, as far as we can tell Henry Ziegland's life was pretty unremarkable until about 1883, when he decided to break up with his fiancée, Maysie Tichnor.

Devastated, Maysie took her own life, unable to live with a broken heart and the sadness that often stems from a failed romance.

Reports indicate that Maysie had an older brother who was naturally upset and angered by the cause of his sister's death. He stormed around to Henry's house and the pair scuffled, which escalated when the brother drew a pistol. He fired a single shot which sizzled past Henry's face, grazing his cheek on the way through before lodging in a nearby pine tree.

What happened next is up for debate, but we're led to believe that after avenging his sister's death – or at least nearly avenging it – the brother turned the pistol on himself.

With two deaths on his conscience, it was time for Henry to lie low, which is precisely what he did. For the next twenty years he kept to himself, pottering around at the same address and quietly getting on with his life. Then in 1903 Henry decided the time had come to freshen up his property, perhaps do a little landscaping.

The first order of business was removing an unsightly tree from his front yard. Now in retrospect, Henry's most significant fuck-up was not employing an arborist to cut down the tree. Instead, Henry would do it himself.

Despite his enthusiasm, Henry lacked the correct gear to bring down the mighty pine properly. Rather than admit defeat, Henry refused to be beaten by a tree and improvised. In what seems like the most Texan-style solution of all time, he strapped sticks of dynamite to the tree trunk and blew it up. The result intended was that the tree would fall, and Henry would live happily ever after. Neither of those things happened.

The firepower of the dynamite did indeed obliterate the tree, but it also dislodged the wayward bullet from twenty years previously, which promptly sped across the lawn and entered Henry's head, killing him instantly.

Two decades after first exiting the gun chamber, the bullet finally found its mark, a full-circle fuck-up that proved disastrously fatal.

It's worth mentioning that the authenticity of Henry's story has been widely debated, with internet sleuths believing it to be a hoax. Proof of the 'patient bullet', as the legend is known, is hard to come by, though newspaper clippings from the time are available to read online.

Either way, it seems a question mark will always hover over Henry Ziegland, the man who proved what goes around does indeed come around, even if it takes a while.

Shit Happens

Author's note
This chapter is made up of three stories that remind us of two indisputable truths: everyone has a horror story about shitting, and everyone finds them funny.

* * * * * *

1 Girl Time

Anna's story
The start of this story reads like the synopsis for a romantic comedy, the kind that Julia Roberts seemed to exclusively star in during the 1990s: *Fresh off the back of a breakup, Anna,*

a studious brunette, moves to France and falls in love with Simon, a charming Englishman.

Anna and Simon first cross paths serendipitously. It's a classic meet-cute moment: Anna is strolling the Champs-Élysées thinking about her broken heart when – *merde!* – she slips in dog shit. Luckily, our leading man, Simon (picture a Hugh Grant type), is on hand to catch her before she falls.

Cue a movie montage of the perfect day – walking, talking, ice cream, flirting – followed by a candlelit dinner. While twirling pasta onto his fork, Simon says something charming like: 'I have a feeling this may be your last first date.'

Hiding the fact she is already head over heels, Anna jokes: 'You think this is a date?'

They spend the night together, and the next night, and the one after that. Fast forward two months, Anna and Simon have not left each other's side; they are in love. So in love that when Simon invites Anna to fly to England and meet his family, she agrees without hesitation.

And this is when our romantic comedy takes a sharp plot twist and starts to more closely resemble a horror movie . . .

* * * * * * *

'You don't need to be nervous,' said Simon, holding the restaurant door open for me, 'they're going to love you!'

Around us, fancy-looking waiters in vests circulated fancy-looking food.

I wasn't nervous, but the subtext to Simon's comments was: *I am a little nervous, perhaps you should be too.* Simon was lovely, but quite posh, which is probably the most English way to describe the English upper class.

Heading home for the weekend, I think Simon feared a glimpse into his privileged upbringing might shatter the facade of our perfect-yet-penniless lives abroad. In Paris, we had no money, but we had each other. It felt romantic to share one croissant for breakfast or split a bottle of cheap wine because it was all we could afford.

'Still or sparkling?' asked one of the fancy waiters. Sparkling, replied Simon, keeping both eyes on the door. We were the first to arrive.

I already suspected that being poor was more of a phase for Simon. He had spoken of his family's summer houses and winter cottages and autumn lodges. I'm not sure where they went in spring, but undoubtedly they had a home for that season too.

'Here they come now,' said Simon, sitting up noticeably straighter as he waved at his mother and father.

Deep down, I knew Simon worried we would return

to Paris *changed*, that seeing his wealth up-close might shift the balance. He was right to worry, but not about the wealth.

'Mother, Father, *this* is Anna,' he said, introducing me to two expensive-looking parents. We shook hands, went through the motions. *We've heard so much about you! Oh, all good things I hope hahaha!*

A few minutes later, his sister, Margot, joined us. She looked like peak-era Kate Moss and had that vaguely uninterested air that people found so interesting.

'I can't believe you're putting up with my brother,' she whispered in my ear conspiratorially, mid-hug. 'More power to you, has he started fake smoking yet?'

She seemed unpleasant; I liked her instantly.

All in all, lunch was enjoyable and refreshingly normal. Simon's parents asked about Paris and scolded him for not calling enough, Margot shared embarrassing stories from his youth for my benefit.

'Must you?' sighed Simon as his sister launched into another anecdote about his infatuation with the family's elderly housekeeper.

The only hint of trouble came towards the end of the meal in the form of stabbing pains in my abdomen. My decision to order the curry was proving to be a bad one, and I could feel it racing through me.

'I just need to use the bathroom,' I said, excusing myself as quickly as possible.

'Wait,' called out Margot, her slender hand gripping me by the forearm. 'I'll join you! Girl time!'

On the walk to the restroom, I panicked about our wildly different intentions. It was apparent Margot was hoping for a besties-in-the-bathroom type of visit. Reapply a little lipstick in the mirror and come out attached at the hip. I had more pressing issues.

We entered the ladies, and there were only two cubicles, one of which was already occupied.

'You said you needed to go, so you go first,' offered Margot.

This should be incredibly awkward, I thought to myself, locking the door.

As tends to happen, the moment I was physically near the toilet things escalated, time was of the essence. The need to go intensified but I feared the acoustics of this tiny bathroom would amplify every sound.

Having only met Simon's fancy Kate Moss sister an hour ago, I wasn't exactly jazzed about her hearing my curry situation unfold. Using the cough technique, which involves coughing each time you push, I managed to muffle the sound. Success!

I'll spare you the details, but considering the gigantic shit I'd taken, I was quietly proud that I'd masked the noise. My relief was short-lived when I flushed, and *of course*, it didn't go down.

Instead, I came face to face with a universal toilet terror: rising water. *Please no, please don't let this be happening.* But then as quickly as the tide rose, it sucked back down violently, leaving a soggy mess behind.

Fuck.

'Everything all right?' asked Margot. It was not.

'Yep, all good!' I said, trying to sound like someone carefree and happy, someone not in this predicament. *GIRL TIME!*

I knew if I could outlast the woman in the cubicle next to me, all my problems would be solved, but with each passing minute, she showed no signs of finishing up.

By the time we crossed the ten-minute mark, I couldn't wait any longer and decided to take matters into my own hands – literally.

In the corner of the toilet, I spied a little wastepaper bin. Fantastic, I would deposit the poo in there. Using reams of toilet paper, I fished him out of the bowl, and packaged him up, making a kind of poop parcel, if you will.

As soon as I was holding the parcel, I knew I'd made a terrible mistake. Disrupting the ecosystem only seemed to increase the stench, and now the entire toilet reeked.

The more I moved around, the more it seemed to spread, and I began to cough and gag on the smell. At least if

I died here, I wouldn't have to face Margot, who was now knocking on the door.

'Anna, what's going on in there?'

'One minute!'

Fuckkk, fuckkk.

A quick check under the cubicle confirmed my next-door neighbour was *still* going at it – *she must've also had the curry* – and my options faded from view. How had a lovely weekend away to meet the family turned into hiding out in a London toilet, holding my own shit?

While pondering this question, I noticed a small window above the toilet. It was barely open, but enough room to slip my hand through.

Of course, there was a risk it might lead to a back alley where the chefs go to smoke or a pleasant outdoor dining courtyard, but it was a risk I had to take.

With one foot on the toilet bowl, I leaned up to the window, parcel in my right hand. Just as I prepared to drop it, Margot knocked again.

'Are you doing what I think you're doing?' came the posh voice from the other side of the door.

I certainly doubt it. 'Ummm, I don't know, am I?'

'Why didn't you tell me?' laughed Margot, followed by the sound of the lock being tampered with. 'I'm coming in!'

No, no, no, no!

SHIT HAPPENS

Here's the scene Margot walked in on: me, a fully grown adult woman, in an expensive restaurant, standing on a toilet, about to launch a wad of wrapped-up shit out a window.

'Oh, my lord! Anna! What is going on!?' She looked confused, mortified and strangely sinister.

'Why did you come in?' I yelled back at her.

'I thought you were doing coke in here! What is that in your hand and why are you standing on the toilet!?'

Before I could answer, she put the pieces together in her head. 'Wait, were you about to – '

'Please Margot,' I begged. 'Never tell anyone?'

'Darling, this is too fantastic,' she said, pulling out her phone and snapping a photo.

'You're hilarious!'

So much for girl time.

* * * * * * *

The ending of this romantic comedy isn't romantic at all.

Simon and Anna fly back to Paris, and before they've even landed at Charles de Gaulle airport, Margot has sent her brother the photo of Anna standing on the toilet. Caught mid-act. The terror is visible on her face, the parcel heavy in her hand.

Anna explains the situation and while Simon laughs in all the right places, says all the right things, she can tell the experience has stained ... ah actually, let's say *tainted* their love. His parents must know, and Simon won't ever let that go.

For a few months, they plod along as before, but it is different now, changed. He cringes every time she goes to use the bathroom.

They break up.

Credits roll.

* * * * * * *

2 The Usual Spot

Hamish's story

They say nothing good happens after two o'clock in the morning, but I reckon they should also warn you that *only* bad things happen after four o'clock in the morning.

'That'll be forty-five dollars and fifty cents,' said the driver, bringing the meter to a stop.

'Aren't you Uber?' I slurred, making no sense.

The cabbie shook his head, the clock on the dashboard read 3:58 am and he had better things to do. 'No, I'm not an Uber, now pay the fare so I can go home.'

Fishing through my wallet I handed over three twenty dollar bills, which he grabbed, looked at briefly and tossed back to me. 'Two Maccas receipts and an out-of-date boat licence for Hamish Riley.'

'Wait, how do you know my name? And where are we?' I asked, packing away the stash I'd given him.

'I don't know mate,' he replied as the clock ticked over to 3.59.

'Your house, your mum's house, Disney-fucking-land, who cares just fix me up. *Real* money this time.'

I passed him what I hoped was an actual fifty dollar note. 'And how did I get here?'

'Some bloke chucked you in the back, gave me the street name and told me to wake you up when we got here.'

'Well thanks, keep the change.'

Stumbling out of the car I checked my phone: low battery and one new message.

Rachel: *Keys are out back in the usual spot.*

This presented three immediate problems that I was far too drunk to be dealing with.

Firstly, I'd only been to Rachel's five or six times before. We were still in the early days, seeing each other on the weekends, maybe once during the week. I had no fucking clue where the usual spot was.

Secondly, I didn't even know which house was hers. Rachel lived in one of those display home suburbs where every house looked the same. White brick, single-storey, laneway down the side.

Particularly unhelpful when you've had 400 beers. Yes, the third and final problem: the beers.

I'd spent the previous eight hours boozing at my footy club's end of season presentation night. Basically, it's just an excuse for weekend warriors to get written off and tell stories about how they *almost* made it.

I usually skip it but this year my mate Harry twisted my arm. 'Free piss and free pizza,' was how he sold it to me. Tough to turn down.

Having gone too hard on both the free piss and pizza I was coming into Rachel's red hot, lurching down the street squinting at the identical houses.

Somewhere in my boozy brain, I remembered Rachel had sent me her address during the evening. I scrolled back through our texts, and bingo, there she was.

Rachel: *For when you forget, it's 21 Roster Street, North Perth x*

With one eye closed, I started punching out a reply on the off-chance Rachel might be awake.

Where is the usual spot?

Before I could hit send the battery flashed and the

screen went to black. The last thing I saw was the time: 4.01 am.

Prime conditions for a total disaster.

****

'Would you rather have Paddle Pop fingers or no fingers at all?' Harry asked earlier that night, cracking two beers and handing one to me.

'Paddle Pop fingers,' I replied.

Given we were rubbish at footy and not a chance of winning an award, Harry had insisted on sitting up the back and playing his favourite game: Would You Rather?

No matter which option I chose, he made it seem like the worst one.

'Paddle Pops for fingers! You're off your head mate. Right, what about this, would you rather eat schnitzel for every meal or never eat schnitzel again?'

'That one's brutal, umm, never again, I guess?'

'You love schnitzel, what's wrong with you?' he snorted. 'Fine, an easy one then. Would you rather be Spiderman for a week or have a year off work?'

It was this last ultimatum that haunted me as I tried, and failed, to scale Rachel's side gate. Spiderman for a week would be handy right about now.

'Shit,' I whispered, falling back on my ass. The gate was made with horizontal aluminium slats and stood a couple of metres high, at least – a real bastard to climb.

Sunrise was a couple of hours off, and it was still dark, but I could make out small gaps between the slats. They were too tight to wedge my shoes into but if I went barefoot, I'd be able to wiggle a couple of toes in and get a foothold.

Kicking off the boots worked a treat and within a couple of minutes I was up and over the gate, facing a fresh obstacle: trip hazards.

Rachel had two flatmates, and like every share house, the side of the house was a dumping ground for ditched hobbies. It required all my concentration not to make a sound as I drunkenly tiptoed past three mountain bikes, a folded-up table-tennis table and a two-person canoe.

By the time I reached the backyard, I was mentally exhausted, but the fun was just beginning: now to find the key.

Rachel's text had read: *keys are out back in the usual spot*, which suggested it was a spot I should know, but glancing around the backyard, nothing looked familiar.

I tried the classic hiding spots first – doormat, inside a shoe, pot plant – but that was a dead-end, so I steered my search to the garden. Like the house next door, and the one next door to that, *and the one next door to that*, this place had a huge grassy area with hedges around the fence line.

One of Rachel's flatmates, Steve, had taken it upon himself to decorate the garden with weird miniature marble statues. I'm not talking about cute garden gnomes in funny hats, I mean like nineteenth-century gothic gargoyles.

Pretty scary stuff, *especially* in the dark, *especially* when you're hammered.

Figuring the creepy gargoyles could be a possible hiding spot, I spent a few minutes looking underneath them when an intense pressure arrived in my rectum.

Next came shooting stomach pains and a low gurgle. Something terrible was happening internally, the free piss and pizza were not getting along and it all added up to one undeniable fact. *I needed to shit.*

'Not good,' I said out loud, pacing and clenching. The search for the key had been abandoned and replaced by a new, more urgent, search: locate backyard bog spot.

The far-left corner of the garden offered the most shelter, so I waddled in that direction, stepping over the sprinkler on the way. Conveniently, someone, probably Steve, had recently laid a fresh layer of topsoil which I was about to add to.

The next part was a low point, and there's no real way to gloss over it. Dropping my pants, I took an emergency shit in Rachel's garden; I soiled her topsoil. The silver lining was that it came out smoothly and quickly, a clean break that didn't require wiping, but if that's the best part of your day then you're having a pretty bad day.

Please know that none of this makes me proud, and please also know there are several lower points just around the corner.

Mid-shit, while quietly contemplating how far I'd fallen, I heard what sounded like a swarm of locusts but was, in fact, Rachel's oscillating high-powered sprinkler system kicking into gear.

It must've been on an automatic timer, and my squat coincided with the moment it switched on, covering the garden, and me, with water.

Having grown up with a father who loved his lawn more than his children, I instantly recognised the sprinkler setting: cycle and soak. Short bursts of high-powered water pressure designed to soak deep into the soil. Good for the roots, bad for people shitting in the garden.

In a panic, I half-pulled up my pants and raced around, frantically trying to find the tap so I could turn the water off. After two laps I realised it was back where I'd started, near my shame potty.

Sidestepping the mess, I twisted the handle, and the sprinkler dribbled to a stop. I was drenched, doubled over and disgraced, but not, as it turned out, defeated. Tucked away behind the tap was a small magnetic box and inside that box was Rachel's house key.

In the usual spot. Apparently.

Once inside the house, I had a solid escape plan: track down a phone charger so I could order an Uber and be on my way.

Rachel's room is a straight shot from the back of the house, third door on the right. I crept down the hallway, thankful for the carpeted floor that muted each footstep.

She was sound asleep when I opened her door, and it took serious willpower not to peel off my wet clothes and jump into the warm bed. Instead, I quietly unplugged the charger and retreated down the hallway.

While waiting for the phone to charge in the kitchen, I scribbled an apology on a spare piece of paper:

Long story short: usual spot confused me!

Sorry, I left, didn't want to wake you. Call me tomorrow.

Finally my phone buzzed back to life and I booked an Uber, falling asleep on the ride home.

* * * * * * *

Would you rather wake up to the shrill voice of your girlfriend explaining that you've stepped in your own shit and walked it through her house, or never wake up at all?

The next morning, I was forced awake by a flurry of notifications coming from my phone. Six missed calls, seven messages and a voicemail from Rachel.

It started like this: 'WHAT HAVE YOU DONE?'

Continued like this: 'SHIT THROUGH THE ENTIRE HOUSE!'

Touched on this: 'DID YOU TAKE A SHIT IN OUR GARDEN?'

And ended like this: 'IT'S FUCKING EVERY-WHERE!'

Even through a heavy hangover, I started to piece together what had happened. While running from the sprinkler I must've stepped in the shit I'd taken. Unfortunately, due to mitigating factors (drunk, dark, I'm a dickhead) I didn't notice, and proceeded to stomp it through Rachel's house.

I would later learn that I'd left a trail of perfectly formed brown footprints on the carpet. You could track my every step, from the back door to Rachel's room, through to the kitchen, and then out the front door.

The phone rang once more, Rachel's name flashed up on the screen, the time was 9.55 am.

Call back in five minutes, I told myself. Nothing bad happens after ten o'clock in the morning.

* * * * * *

3 A Shitshow in Shinjuku

Prologue

It's 2009 and four friends – Lucas, Anthony, Sam and Ryan – go out for a fancy dinner in Tokyo.

After three weeks of travelling together, it's their final night in town. During the course of the evening, an incident occurs, and they agree to never speak about it again. Until now.

* * * * * * *

PART I: THE DINNER

Anthony's story

The first sign of trouble came with the DIY surf and turf. It wasn't even on the menu, but Ryan decided to order both the lobster tail and the steak, then combine the two.

'Is it possible to get them served on the same plate?' he asked.

The waiter, confused but accommodating, nodded slowly. 'And for you, sir?'

'I'll have the burger please.' I was broke, and at Park Hyatt prices I couldn't afford much else.

'I'll have the burger too,' echoed also-broke Lucas.

'Actually, I might try the lobster tail and steak,' said Sam, as though it were a real dish, not one Ryan had made up minutes ago.

It was our last supper and in a classic case of *be careful what you wish for* we were determined to finish the trip with an *unforgettable night*.

I'd suggested the Park Hyatt because I loved the movie *Lost in Translation*. You know the one: Bill Murray mopes around Tokyo and eventually Scarlett Johansson falls in love with him. The film was shot in the hotel, and I liked the idea of sitting where Bill Murray had once sat.

It was Sam's call to get dressed up for the occasion, really go all out. He wore a vest, Lucas and I bought knitted bow ties, and Ryan debuted his brand-new electric blue patent leather shoes that cost more than I made in a month.

On reflection, we looked ridiculous, like a bloated barber-shop quartet, but at the time it felt special.

'A toast,' said Lucas, raising his glass of free tap water. 'To three weeks with three of the best.'

We cheersed to our holiday as the food arrived, the surf and turf looking unlike anything I'd seen coughed up by an RSL back home.

'Easily the best and *only* surf and turf I've had in Japan,' declared Sam.

'Yeah, not bad,' said Ryan unconvincingly. 'Though I do feel a little funny in the tummy, pretty rich, don't you reckon?'

This comment was a sign of things to come but not a sign that we should worry. For the entire trip, Ryan had provided constant and hourly updates on his troublesome tummy. Not a meal went by without him clutching at his midsection and asking everyone else how they felt. I put his sensitivity down to the fact he never ate leftovers growing up, so he didn't have good gut bacteria.

'You should go and sit on the toilet,' I said. 'Even if you don't need to, honestly mate, best toilet I've ever sat on.'

This was no exaggeration; I'd visited the bathrooms earlier and been blown away. Like shitting in a ballroom.

'He's right,' said Lucas, returning from his own visit. 'Fucking immaculate in there, a highlight of the trip for me.'

After hearing the wrap on the toilets, Sam's fear of missing out kicked in and he rushed to check them out, but Ryan remained rooted to the spot.

'I really don't need to go,' he said, lowering his voice. 'I actually haven't been in six days.'

As a three-a-day-like-clockwork kinda guy this revelation was shocking to me, but each to their own. We paid the bill, Sam and Ryan shelling out handsomely for their made-up mains.

By the time we jumped in the lift, I could see Ryan massaging his stomach and shifting on the spot. He looked uncomfortable, and I remember thinking, 'This guy is gonna need to go soon, and we're about to walk away from the best toilet facilities in the wider Tokyo area.'

****

PART II: THE INCIDENT

Ryan's story

Not shitting for six days is a lot like coming to terms with a shocking death in that you progress through the five stages of grief.

First comes denial. Six days? No way it's been six days. Wait, what's the date?

Then anger. SIX GODDAMN DAYS!

Then bargaining. Okay look, if I eat right when I get home, and exercise every day, will you just give me a pellet, a spurt, something!

Next depression. What's the point of doing shit, if you can't actually do a shit?

And finally acceptance. Backed up, but never broken.

Heading out for our farewell dinner in Tokyo, I was hovering around acceptance when the surf and turf sent mayday signals through my system. It hit me hard in the lift, and I remember Anthony sussing me out; he could tell it was a serious predicament.

By the time we reached the ground floor, I could feel a six-day build just knock-knock-knocking on my back door.

'Honestly mate, you need to get back in that lift, and go use the bathroom,' said Anthony.

I probably should've listened, but at the time, the idea of heading back to that swanky restaurant, finding our poor waiter and being like, 'Hey mate, I hear the bathrooms are fucking immaculate here, do you mind if I put that to the test?' was not appealing.

Instead, I was determined to find a public bathroom for my private shame.

'Guys, wait here I'll be ten minutes tops,' were my final words as I headed off into the wilds of Shinjuku.

The Park Hyatt borders the business district of Shinjuku, so it was mostly office buildings with no signs of life, but at first, I didn't feel that stressed. I think in a situation like this you convince yourself that the worst-case scenario won't ever happen.

Five minutes passed, and the panic levels picked up, one hand gently cupping my bottom, but even then, I was sure I'd find a toilet, like *surely* in a city of nine million, a city where nothing is left to chance, there will be a toilet.

But it was quite late by this point, maybe 10 pm, and everything was closed for business, except for my anus, which seemed to be opening for the first time in a week.

After another five minutes, the situation skyrocketed from *dearie me* to *absolutely dire*, and I resorted to harassing anyone who crossed my path.

'EXCUSE ME, *SUMIMASEN*,' I yelled at one old lady. 'TOILET?'

She abused me in Japanese and pointed in the direction of a bridge. My gut told me this was wrong, but my gut also thought lobster and steak was a smart idea, so I didn't trust it.

I started a movement best described as 'jog-waddling', and while I don't recall how far I got, I do remember the moment it struck. The moment I knew I wasn't going to make it.

Ten metres out from the bridge, my jog slowed to a walk and finally to a stop. All I could do was repeat the words *'it's here'* as six days' worth of backed up shit ballooned into my pants. To make matters worse, they were incredibly tight, skinny leg jeans and they literally filled to the brim, as if someone had released compressed air in them, like when you rapidly inflate a jumping castle.

Instant volume.

Taking refuge under the bridge, I was trying to compose myself when I noticed my shoes. That same day I'd bought these obscene electric blue patent leather dress shoes for

$1000, and now they were reduced to obscene electric blue patent poo-holders. Ruined on first wear.

You may think you've felt hopeless, but until you've been forced to hide in the darkness in the middle of Tokyo, jeans and shoes full of shit, you don't know what it means to scrape the bottom of the barrel.

Thank the lord I had global roaming on my phone, so I called Sam and kept it brief – 'Mate, I've shit myself' – then explained where I was and hung up, alone with my thoughts and soiled outfit.

I've often wondered what might've happened if I hadn't had my phone on me that night. Maybe I'd still be there, flinging shit at people under the bridge. Beware the Tokyo Troll.

The thought haunts me to this day.

* * * * * * *

PART III: THE CLEAN-UP

Lucas's story
There's never been a more impeccable example of comic timing than Ryan calling with the poo news.

He'd been gone just long enough for one us to wonder out loud, 'Where the fuck is Ryan?' and at that exact moment he rang Sam and said, 'Mate, I've shit myself under a bridge'.

As soon as we heard the words, Sam, Anthony and I hit the deck in hysterics, dropping as if a gun had gone off. Can't speak, can't breathe kind of laughter, when the more you look at each other, the longer it lasts. I love that.

Using the instructions Ryan gave Sam, we tracked down the weird grotto he was hiding in.

Even now I can picture the look on his face when we turned up: so defeated. The whole image was heartbreaking and hilarious. It didn't help that Ryan is six foot two with red hair; the tallest, saddest, stinkiest man in Tokyo.

He clearly needed help, so we decided to split up into teams, Anthony and I were on cleaning supplies, and Sam covered the change of clothes.

I'd love to know what the guy working at 7-Eleven made of our purchase: six two-litre bottles of water, three rolls of toilet paper and five bars of soap at 11 pm.

'Is that everything?' he asked, bagging the clean-up goods.

'That should do it,' I told him.

Meanwhile, Sam was proving that he's the man you need in a crisis. He had sprinted down to the Tokyo Hilton and spun an elaborate story about how his wife was about to give birth in the back of a taxi and he needed some pyjamas to mop up the placenta. It was bonkers, but they bought it, or more likely, they just wanted him to get off the premises.

We reconvened and handed our assignments to Ryan, who retreated into the shadows to clean himself up.

'Do you reckon he's going to be okay?' Anthony asked.

'Do you reckon any of us will be?' replied Sam.

My thoughts mostly went out to whichever unfortunate City of Tokyo cleaner stumbled across that disaster scene the next morning. Bottles of water, soap bars, a pair of blue patent leather shoes full of shit, you don't bounce back from that.

After a few minutes, Ryan emerged, barefoot and in his white pyjamas, looking like a cult leader.

Understandably, he was keen to get home, so he hurried past us to the taxi rank, and that was when I glimpsed it: the most enduring image of our Japanese holiday. At some point during the wipe down Ryan must've dried his hands on the back of his pyjamas, leaving two perfect light brown handprints across the buttocks.

Fantastic.

* * * * * * *

PART IV: THE CAB RIDE

Sam's story

Japan is the politest place on earth, hands down; you won't find a country where people are more polite. In Japan, you could shoot someone in the head and they would apologise for getting in the way of your bullet.

So when we piled into the taxi, one of us clearly reeking of shit, I wasn't surprised when the driver remained silent. Polite to a fault, he just kept his eyes on the road, blinking away tears, and breathing through the mouth. The closest he came to expressing any kind of dissatisfaction was simultaneously winding down all four automatic windows.

'Very warm,' he said as the sub-zero winds sent a chill through the car.

No one spoke for most of the trip, but as we neared our hotel, Ryan broke the silence to demand a vow of silence.

'Guys,' he said, sounding serious. He was sitting up front while Ant, Lucas and I rode in the back. 'I know you probably think that when enough time has passed, in a few years, and this is water under the –' *don't say bridge* '– bridge, we'll be able to look back at this and laugh. But that's not the case, can we please promise to never, *ever*, talk of this again?'

'No worries, of course, mate, definitely,' came the rush of assurance from the back seat.

We pulled up at our stop, Ryan emptying all the yen in his wallet onto the driver's lap, before sprinting inside to shower forever.

'Surely, we'll be able to tell people one day?' asked Ant, a grin on his face.

'Eventually we will,' I said. 'Some stories are too good not to share.'

THE F*** UP HALL OF FAME

Emu Warfare

> **Name**: The Australian Army   **Rating**: 5/10
>
> **Fuck-up**: An official military operation to wipe out troublesome emus in Western Australia: what could possibly go wrong?

If you've ever actually read Sun Tzu's *The Art of War*, then chances are you work in middle management and are desperate to impress your boss. Or maybe you've just got too much time on your hands.

However, in between the vague pieces of life advice that sound like Insta-quotes from your favourite influencer – 'Opportunities multiply as they are seized!' – the book does contain a few valuable lessons.

One point Tzu hammers home is that you should never underestimate your opponent: 'He who exercises no forethought but makes light of his opponents is sure to be captured by them,' writes Tzu.

Basically, he's saying that to avoid paying the ultimate price, you must pay respect to your enemy. Even if that enemy is an emu.

Some context: in the aftermath of World War I, state and federal governments set up the Soldier Settlement Scheme, designed to resettle returned soldiers on the land.

In Western Australia, more than 5000 soldiers were allocated farmland, a kind of agricultural 'thank you for your service'. But in 1932, in the depths of the Great Depression, the soldiers encountered an enemy far more significant than any they had faced overseas: the native emu.

Drought had turned Australia's favourite flightless bird (take that, cassowary!) into a costly pest. Driven by a search for water, 20,000-odd emus began trampling crops in Western Australia, demolishing wheat stocks and leaving a trail of destruction in their wake.

Eventually, the emu invasion became so bad that the military was called to intervene, with Defence minister George Pearce sanctioning an official military operation. Unofficially dubbed 'the Great Emu War', this operation quickly became a great farce, and an even greater fuck-up.

Led by Major G.P.W. Meredith, commander of the Royal Australian Artillery's Seventh Heavy Battery, the plan was to gun down the emus using Lewis machine guns, which had proved effective during World War I. The Lewis was capable of holding almost 100 rounds and firing 500 rounds per minute.

With 10,000 bullets at his disposal, Major Meredith expected a comfortable victory. What match was an emu for the might and power of the army?

Beginning in October 1932, the Great Emu War got off to a shaky start. First, the emus proved to be far smarter than anyone had given them credit for. They soon worked out the range of the Lewis gun, staying far enough away that the bullets wouldn't reach them. This forced Major Meredith to employ ambush attacks, but again the birds were one step ahead. Using tactics that would make Sun Tzu beam with delight, the emus would splinter into small groups, making it near-impossible for the army to wipe them all out.

The longer the Emu War dragged on, the more obvious it became to everyone involved who had the upper hand, or in this case, claw.

'The emus have proved that they are not so stupid as they are usually considered to be,' the *Kalgoorlie Miner* newspaper reported on 5 November 1932. 'Each mob has its leader, who keeps watch while his fellows busy themselves with the wheat. At the first suspicious sign, he gives the signal, and dozens of heads stretch out of the crop.'

After months of chasing shadows through the Australian outback, the powers that be demanded a ceasefire on 8 November. Official records indicate that from 10,000 bullets, the army had only registered 986 feathered fatalities, meaning it took roughly ten bullets to take down a single emu.

In late 1932, Pearce pressured parliament to allow the Emu War to resume, but public frustration was mounting and his appeal was denied.

The Emu War was over. The feathered foe had mastered the art of war and come out on top.

Acknowledgments

In a year that was defined by a need to keep our distance, I feel lucky to have written a book that allowed me to connect with so many people about memorable moments from their lives. Sure, those moments were mortifying, painful, embarrassing and hilarious, but it was a timely reminder that, at the end of the day, we all just crave connection.

Thank you to everyone who shared so generously. This experience has taught me that our personal stories have real currency, so I'll be forever grateful to those brave souls who contributed their best (and worst) moments. I hope I did you all justice.

To my publisher, Emma Nolan, the first person to give me a proper job – even though I was hopeless at buying cakes – and the first person to convince me I could write a book. Thank you for always pushing me in the right direction.

Thank you to my close friends and family. Like most writers, I live my life by committee, desperate for the thoughts of my nearest and dearest. During this process, you have all proven to be outstanding sounding boards, and I'm sorry for abusing that privilege.

Thank you to my book club of two, Caitlin and Ryan. Your words of wisdom and schooners of beer proved crucial ingredients in the making of this work, and the surviving of several meltdowns.

To my wife, Kate, who is at the heart and soul of everything I do, f***ing up is the most fun when you're involved. I love you.

And finally to Ian O'Connor, the man who drove me to write this book. Quite literally.

About the Author

After continually being told to 'use his words' as a child, Thomas Mitchell took that advice on board and ran with it. Since then his words have appeared all over the place, including in *The Sydney Morning Herald*, *Time Out*, *The Huffington Post*, *The New York Times* and *GQ*. A full-time writer, Thomas spends his days googling synonyms and trying not to overstay his welcome at the local cafe.